The
BOBBY JONES
Way

The BOBBY JONES *Way*

How To Apply The Swing Secrets of Golf's All-Time Power-Control Player To Your Own Game

John Andrisani

HarperResource
An Imprint of HarperCollins*Publishers*

HarperCollins books may be purchased for educational, business, or sales promotional use. For information please write: Special Markets Department, Harper-Collins Publisher Inc., 10 East 53rd Street, New York, NY 10022.

FIRST HARPERRESOURCE PAPERBACK EDITION PUBLISHED 2004

Designed by Mary Austin Speaker
Illustrations by Shu Kuga
Photographs by Yasuhiro Tanabe

The Library of Congress has Catalogued the hardcover edition as follows:

Andrisani, John.
    The Bobby Jones way: swing secrets of golf's all-time power-control player /
    John Andrisani.–1st ed.
        p. cm.
Includes index.
ISBN 0-06-018515-5
1. Swing (Golf) 2. Jones, Bobby 1902-1971. I. Title

GV979.S9 A525 2002
796.352'3–dc21

ISBN 0-06-095976-2 (pbk.)

04   05   06   07 08 ❖ / RRD   10   9   8   7   6   5   4   3   2   1

I dedicate this book to golfers across the world who are ready to trade their inconsistent swing in for a natural-flowing action like the one used by the great Bobby Jones.

Contents

Acknowledgments

As the author of *The Bobby Jones Way,* only my byline appears on the cover, yet I am indebted to other individuals for their hard work and support. One such person is the late Charles Price, who during one lengthy nineteenth-hole session in Scotland, nearly two decades ago, shared with me anecdotes about Jones and valuable opinions on what he believed were Jones's swing secrets. Price, a former editor at *GOLF Magazine* and, of course, a Jones swing disciple, as well as a friend to Jones, wrote the foreword and edited a revised edition of one of Jones's most noteworthy instruction books, *Bobby Jones on Golf,* printed in 1966. Price, who played what is today the PGA Tour as an amateur in 1947 and 1948, is best remembered for this comment: "I retired from competition at the age of twenty-eight, the same age as Bobby Jones. The difference was that Jones retired because he beat everybody and I retired because I couldn't beat anybody." Actually, having played St. Andrews with "Charlie," I can attest that he was an excellent golfer and great student of the game. I owe him tremendous gratitude for his input. I only wish he were alive, so that I could share with him my own newly discovered swing and shot-making secrets Jones never mentioned.

This book would never have been published had it not been for two New York City–based professionals: Scott Waxman, of the Scott Waxman Agency, and Matthew Benjamin, my editor at HarperCollins Publishers. Both believed strongly in my idea to analyze the techniques of the man considered by many golf experts around the world to be the smoothest swinger of all time: Robert Tyre (Bobby) Jones.

I'm also grateful for the wonderfully lifelike drawings of Jones done by Shu Kuga, an award-winning artist, since they certainly help put across the instructional points presented in the text that follows.

The photographs in this book also help relay the instructional message and add to its nostalgic flavor. Therefore, I thank Allsport and Gavin Darbyshire for supplying vintage photographs, and Yasuhiro Tanabe for his additional course shots.

With respect to the focal point of *The Bobby Jones Way*, the Jones swing and shot-making analysis, I thank top-rated instructors who appear on lists put out by both *GOLF Magazine* and *Golf Digest*. I'm also grateful to members of the United States Golf Teachers Federation, tour professionals, television golf commentators, members of the golf press, and low-handicap amateur golfers for their views on Jones.

Special thanks to Sybervision, for the video *The Bobby Jones Instructional Series*, showing reminiscent footage of Jones's classic swing techniques, produced by Warner Brothers in 1931 and 1932. Every golfer should have this tape in his or her library, because when you watch it, you feel that you are taking lessons from the man himself. I know I did. Watching this video helped me analyze Jones's swing and determine some of his true swing and shot-making secrets.

Before sharing Jones's secrets with you, I must thank the immortal Bobby Jones himself, who I suspect is in heaven hitting drives down the fairway and irons dead to the stick. I thank him for his exceptional talent, on-course etiquette, off-course manners, generosity in giving back to golf, and the spirit he brought to the game, near and afar, yesterday, today, and tomorrow.

Introduction

When I first set out researching *The Bobby Jones Way,* I reread books written by Robert Tyre (Bobby) Jones and about him. I also studied photographs and videotape showing Jones swinging, with the intention of determining his swing secrets—keys to his ball-striking and shot-making prowess that Jones himself never mentioned in his writings.

In looking for clues to solving the mystery of Jones's swing, I was guided considerably by the Sybervision tape, as I have acknowledged previously. What I didn't tell you is that the final segment of the video features slow-motion footage of Jones swinging, with no commentary from Jones. There must be some truth to the cliché "Silence is golden," because the lack of any voice-over helped me concentrate more intently and figure out Jones's technical secrets that are about to be revealed to you.

The Bobby Jones Way is presented in a similar critical-analysis fashion as two other swing-analysis books I have written that continue to be well received by readers like yourself: *The Tiger Woods Way* and *The Hogan Way.* In addition to my own commentary about the swing and shot-making techniques of Jones, there will be comments from top teachers, including John Anselmo, Tiger's teacher from the age of ten to eighteen, and Butch Harmon, Tiger's present teacher. I also depend on other golf notables, such as equipment expert Nick Mastroni.

There is a passion for Jones, and a curiosity about his technique, as there is for Ben Hogan and Tiger Woods. One thing sets Jones apart, however. He played golf in an era when clubshafts were constructed from hickory wood, and thus flexible. Ironically, the steel and graphite shafts of today that are marked "stiff" or "firm flex" by manufacturers are also *soft*. Many of the winners on the PGA Tour swing clubs that bend pretty much like Jones's hickory-shaft clubs. Club-makers are returning to more flexible shafts because they know they give golfers more feel for the clubhead and are more manageable. This design feature is truly an asset because it allows you to swing the club more smoothly, like Jones, and pick up more distance just by timing the snap of the shaft at impact.

Jones employed a swing that was nothing less than poetic, yet surprisingly many golfers, particularly the most youthful, are unaware of him and the intricate elements that made his wonderful swing work so rhythmically and produce a variety of shots.

Most of the books written by Jones or about Jones chronicle his tournament life and achievements. Besides, the limited number of books containing solid instruction are long out of print and so very rare that they are expensive if you are lucky enough to locate one from a collector or at auction. Furthermore, the most recent books on Jones, such as the elegantly presented and wonderfully written *Bobby Jones: The Greatest of Them All*, track his competitive life as an amateur, yet devote a limited number of pages to Jones's swing technique.

In conducting my research further for *The Bobby Jones Way*, I discovered that even though many golf historians and swing gurus consider Jones's swing the purest of all time, no golf-magazine or book writer had ever before tried to tap into his true secrets. Again, I am not talking about what Jones knew and said he did, I'm talking about what he never talked about or refrained from talking about for reasons of secrecy.

I feel strongly that *The Bobby Jones Way* delivers on its promise to reveal Jones's swing and shot-making secrets that were never revealed in books, magazine articles, or in instructional films produced in Hollywood and shown in movie theaters throughout the country during the 1930s. For example, when discussing the setup, I focus on the unique way Jones gripped the club. Jones pressed a substantial portion of his right thumb against the tip of his right forefinger to promote feel and control of the clubhead. This was a secret he failed to share but one that made a big difference to his shot-making prowess and will to yours. Also, rather than set both hands on the club in a neutral position that's commonly recommended by teachers, and by Jones himself, he actually held the club with quite a strong left-hand grip and a weak right-hand grip.

I also observed that Jones kept moving some part of his body before he actually started to swing, which to the best of my knowledge, is something Jones never talked about. Jones could either be seen gripping and regripping the club, jockeying his feet into position, focusing his eyes several times from ball to target, or tilting his left hip higher than his right hip. This constant movement helped Jones stay relaxed and promoted a smooth transition from the setup position to the swing. Golfers who freeze over the ball—and many amateurs suffer from this fault—will profit greatly by copying Jones.

Babe Bellagamba, of the United States Golf Teachers Federation, noticed that when Jones employed a smooth take-away action, the clubhead lagged behind his body and arms. When most recreational golfers swing, the clubhead is first to go. In Jones's case, it was last. This "lag swing," not talked about in any detail by Jones, is what Bellagamba believes was Jones's secret to creating a strong hip turn, a wide swing arc, and power. This makes sense when you consider that Jones was one of the longest hitters of his day despite his small stature.

In analyzing Jones's technique, I also observed that Jones swung the club beyond parallel and pointed the club slightly right of target, which, by the way, is now a new trend among PGA Tour players. The short backswing is history; even Tiger Woods has gone back to a long backswing.

On the way down, Jones was also masterful and savvy. He worked his left foot in a unique way that will be explained in chapter 3 when discussing other swing keys and relating them to equipment. Again, today's clubshafts have play in them, like the hickory shafts of Jones's day. This is precisely why an increasing number of golf instructors are teaching recreational players to use more hand and wrist action, just as Jones did during his heyday. This type of swing technique allows you to feel the clubhead and increase clubhead speed, which are two prerequisites to hitting powerfully accurate shots.

The Bobby Jones Way will include instructional insights that go far beyond the elements of the swing and will thus serve as your guidebook to improvement. This book will trace Jones's learning process. Additionally, it will teach you how to hit creative shots, including Jones's bread-and-butter supercontrolled power draw, and provide you with an analysis of his pitching, chipping, and putting techniques so you save vital strokes during a round of eighteen holes. I will also look at what was so special about Jones's course-management skills and teach you how to cure swing and shot-making problems on the practice tee the way Jones did, so you become a more complete player and enjoy the game more.

The
BOBBY JONES

Way

1 GETTING A GOOD EDUCATION

The origin of Bobby Jones's masterful game

In 1930, Robert Tyre Jones Jr., a twenty-eight-year-old golfer nicknamed Bobby, won the British Amateur, British Open, United States Open, and United States Amateur golf championships. This sweep of all four majors, the Impregnable Quadrilateral, was a tremendous feat. In fact, I believe it remains to this day what esteemed golf writer Herbert Warren Wind, formerly of *The New Yorker* and *Sports Illustrated* magazines, called it, "the greatest single achievement by an athlete in sports history." Jones had "done it all," said ABC-television golf commentator Peter Alliss. This accomplishment was Jones's reward for all the hard work he had put into the game over the years, starting at age six when he spent hundreds of hours hitting shots at Atlanta's East Lake Country Club. There, Jones spent many solitary days perfecting swing and shot-making techniques he learned from Stewart Maiden, the Scottish-born golf professional Bobby often followed around the East Lake course.

The young Bobby Jones, shown here swinging a cut-down brassie club (2-wood), seemed to be born with a great golf technique.

In 1907, when Jones was five years old, his family moved to a house about one hundred yards from East Lake's second fairway. Initially, Jones caught the golf bug after swinging a cut-down cleek (4-wood) given to him by Fulton Colville, one of the club's members. To satisfy his appetite for golf, practically every day Jones and neighbor Frank Meador Jr. played a two-hole course they had designed in front of Meador's parents' home.

In 1908, the Jones family moved to a second golf-course house where Bobby could again see from his window players hitting golf shots. By midyear Bobby had added a brassie (2-wood), cut down from one of his mother's clubs, and a mashie (5-iron), abandoned by his father, to his bag.

During the summer months Jones played almost every day with his mother and father. In the evenings, after supper, he had more fun hitting short pitch shots to the thirteenth green, situated practically in his backyard. Practice paid off; Jones won the first competition he ever entered, a six-hole tournament at East Lake arranged by Mr. Frank Meador. The players Jones beat were Frank Meador Jr., Perry Adair, another golf prodigy, and Alexa Stirling, a neighborhood girl who went on to win many prestigious golf tournaments, including three national women's championships. Jones, at the youthful age of six, won his second tournament at East Lake, too, beating Adair in the final.

Luckily for Jones, he lived on the lip of East Lake and could watch Maiden play. Maiden, whom Jones used as a model and mentor, gave Jones his first full set of hickory clubs so that he could quickly develop a more well-rounded shot-making game, shoot lower scores, and win more tournaments. This was quite a relationship. Jones idolized Maiden because of his pro status and the virtually effortless, technically sound swing he employed. Maiden could see that Jones showed promise so he took control by giving him every advantage. His gift of a new set of clubs, perfectly suited to young Bobby's physique and physical strengths, was surely a step in the right direction.

In 1911, at age nine, Jones won his first big cup, the AAC Junior Championship, beating sixteen-year-old Howard Thorne by a 5-and-4 margin. The photograph in *American Golfer Magazine,* showing victorious little Bobby next to the tall runner-up, turned out to be a harbinger of things to come. Throughout his illustrious competitive career, albeit a short one, Jones was known as the most feared on-course killer.

Jones's enthusiasm for golf grew at a rapid speed and reached great heights in 1913. That summer he watched English professional golfers Harry Vardon and Ted Ray play matches against Maiden and his pro partner Willie Mann at the East Lake and Brookhaven golf courses. And, no doubt, learned some secrets to hitting new shots.

Ironically, though Jones admired this foursome of golfers, adults were admiring his own unique shot-making skills. Jones's distance off the tee surprised most, particularly because he was of small stature. His ability to swing the club powerfully was aided by the strong hands he had inherited from his father, who would have become a professional baseball player had his own dad not put a stop to it. The other reason for

Jones's power was that his swing was a virtual clone of Maiden's. Jones learned to beautifully coordinate the movement of the body with the movement of the club in a wonderfully poetic manner. Moreover, his swing produced shots that hit the most narrow fairways and smallest greens, which is why by age nine he began shooting scores in the 70s. Even more impressively, in 1916, at age fourteen, Jones became the Georgia State amateur champion. The following year, at age fifteen, he won the Southern Amateur.

As good as these accomplishments were, the best was yet to come. Jones's "fat" years, according to traveling companion and biographer Oscar Bane Keeler, began in 1923 when he won the U.S. Open in a play-off against Bobby Cruickshank. Jones's brilliant long-iron hit off a bare lie over water to the heart of the green at the last hole is part of golfing legend.

Jones won the 1924 U.S. Amateur and the same title in 1925 thanks largely to learning the secrets to driving accuracy, on-target shot-making, and a solid short game by watching Maiden play. Although Jones never took formal, hour-long lessons from Maiden, as Tiger Woods did from California-based teaching professional John Anselmo from the age of ten until eighteen, Jones did receive help from him when his swing was really out of sync. The classic example: On the day before the 1925 U.S. Open was to begin, at the Worcester Country Club in Worcester, Massachusetts, Jones was hitting wild shots and feeling panic in his heart when Maiden came to the rescue. Watching Jones hit practice shots, Maiden simply asked Jones, "Why don't you try hitting balls with your backswing?" This cryptic message told Jones he was failing to finish his backswing and, as a result, was swinging down too fast. The tip worked. Jones finished second in this coveted major championship.

In 1926, Jones really broke through, beating the game's best professionals in the U.S. Open and British Open. This was the first time any golfer had won both these coveted championships in the same year.

In 1927, Maiden left East Lake for New York City to set up an indoor teaching school, but not before analyzing his top student's technique.

Jones's unique right-pinky position played a major role in promoting good golf shots.

Maiden checked that Jones let his right pinky rest between the left hand's forefinger and index finger, since this position promotes unification and security in the hands and ultimately helps you return the clubface squarely to the ball and target at impact. He also made sure Jones took a narrow stance and played the ball off his forward foot to encourage a solid upswing hit. Maiden wanted Jones to employ a free and full body turn, with the backswing and downswing blending into one flowing motion. Most important, on the way down, he liked to see Jones's left hand lead the club into impact and the right hand provide the power. Maiden's tune-up paid great dividends. That same year Jones won the U.S. Amateur, defeating Chick Evans in the final, and the British Open, beating a strong field of professionals.

In 1928, Jones won the U.S. Amateur for the fourth time, in 1929 the U.S. Open trophy for the third time, and in 1930, playing discernibly better golf than ever before due to heavy spring practice, the Impregnable Quadrilateral or Grand Slam, as many golf experts call it. By winning the Slam, Jones sat on the highest pedestal, on top of the golf world as an immortal figure looking down at the pros he had beaten.

Jones was the ultimate stylist. Most of all, Jones's technique was natural, owing to active footwork, exaggerated hip rotation, and fluid hand action. Jones also swung the club more like the Scottish champions of days gone by—on a flatter angle or plane with the toe of the club leading the heel at impact. Jones's swinging action allowed him to hit a super-controlled power draw off the tee, and because this shot flies low and rolls more, it gave him a distinct advantage when playing in wind or on a long course.

At this juncture, I feel committed to tell you about the importance of footwork, even though this important fundamental of Jones's swing will be discussed in detail later.

For some reason, Jones downplayed footwork, which does not make sense at all. Some experts believe he did this because he took it for granted that, like Maiden, all golfers lifted their left foot off the ground and replanted it at the start of the downswing. But, to me, this doesn't make much sense either. All Jones had to do was analyze the mechanics of other fine amateurs and professional golfers, too, and he would quickly have determined that many swing flat-footed. This was one reason their swings were out of sync. As Tiger Woods's teacher Butch Harmon told me, "If you want your swing to be rhythmic, start from the ground up."

I believe that Jones believed footwork to be the secret link to blending the backswing and downswing together as one flowing motion and hitting powerful shots, but wanted desperately to keep this vital element a secret. I say this because of a lengthy conversation I had in the middle 1980s, with the late, great professional golfer Harry Cooper, a contemporary of Jones's.

Cooper told me that, prior to the 1927 U.S. Open, Jones gave him a lesson on footwork and assured him that he should try letting the left foot lift high off the ground. According to Cooper, he actually felt embarrassed lifting the left heel up so high, as if some kind of ballet

Superb footwork was a quality of Jones's motion that allowed him to swing the club rhythmically.

dancer, until Jones explained to him that it was not only far more natural a move but a proven secret to generating added clubhead speed.

To prove his point, Jones had Cooper swing the club up and down with his left foot glued to the turf. Next, he had Cooper swing his own way, only lifting the left foot slightly off the ground on the backswing. Last, he had Cooper swing to the top with all but the toe end of the left foot off the ground, pause, then replant his left foot and start rolling weight over to the left heel and outward portion of the left foot. If you try this same experiment, you will feel what Cooper felt: the higher you lift the left heel on the backswing and the faster you replant it on the downswing, the more clubhead speed you generate and the farther you hit the ball. Incidentally, Cooper tied for first in the U.S. Open that year, but lost in a play-off to Jones's friend Tommy Armour, another left-heel lifter.

Jones was the ultimate planner and percentage player who depended on a keen ability to read a lie and a vivid imagination to hit creative shots. He glanced at the ball sitting on fairway grass, rough, or sand and instantly determined exactly how the ball was going to react in the air and on the ground. In an uncanny fashion, he could also make compen-

On chip shots, Jones depended on active lower-body action to help propel the ball to the hole.

satory adjustments during the swing, so on the rare occasion when he started the club on the wrong path, he could usually put it back on track by using his "educated hands."

Contrary to popular belief, Jones's shot-making skills had more to do with practicing with one club as a boy rather than innate talents. By opening and closing the face of a 5-iron, choking down or up on the shaft, setting his hands ahead or behind the ball, and alternating between active hands and wrists and quiet hands and wrist action, he learned to improvise.

Around the greens, Jones was a master who believed in rolling the ball to the hole like a putt, rather than hitting the shot most of the way in the air. His strategy was simple: use an 8-iron on short chips, a medium iron on long chips, and keep the swing simple and natural-feeling.

In setting up to chip, Jones took an open stance, since this helps you see the line more clearly and swing more freely through the ball. In making the backswing, Jones's action was compact, and he allowed the wrists to hinge freely. Wrist action helps you swing the club on an upright plane and ultimately hit down on the ball and also enhances your feel for the clubhead. Since Jones knew where the clubhead was at all times during the swing, he had more control over the shot. On the downswing, he depended on active lower-body action and a hit-and-hold technique through impact to help propel the ball toward the hole the proper distance.

On the greens, Jones used a semi-wristy stroke, as opposed to a pure arms-shoulders action. His secret to hitting the ball on the correct line was to dramatically bend his arms at the elbow, so much so that they pointed practically straight out chicken-wing style. He also rested his right forearm and elbow gently against the body. Jack Nicklaus, who

Bending the arms and pointing both elbows outward helped Jones swing the putter back and through correctly and hit on-line putts.

idolized Jones, copied this style of setting up to putt and claims he uses his "right elbow as a sort of guide, in a sort of pistonlike action, during the stroke." Obviously, this was a smart move, since throughout his career Nicklaus has holed thousands of winning putts.

When reviewing Jones's remarkable shot-making skills and winning record, one must consider the role luck played. Jones was fortunate to have met such a pure swinger as Maiden and to have him for a model and mentor. Jones was also lucky to have grown up playing the East Lake course, redesigned by Donald Ross, and later on, Sara Bay (originally Whitfield Estates Country Club), another Ross course located in Sarasota, Florida. Sara Bay was a favorite of baseball legends Babe Ruth and Dizzy Dean, and other great golfers such as Walter Hagen, Gene Sarazen, Jim Barnes, Johnny Farrell, and Tommy Armour.

In 1926, at age twenty-four, Jones played Sara Bay frequently while

One of Jones's favorite courses was Sara Bay, in Sarasota, Florida, formerly called Whitfield Estates Country Club and designed by legendary architect Donald Ross. Here's Jones, hands in pockets, standing in front of the Sara Bay clubhouse, circa 1926, with some of his fellow champions, including Jim Barnes (far left), Johnny Farrell (third from left), and Tommy Armour (far right).

Tommy Armour, the first golf professional at Sara Bay,
was one of Jones's swing and shot-making mentors.

selling real estate part-time, and in his classic book, *Down the Fairway,*
he called the course "one of the best in America."

What's interesting is that Jones played much of his golf at Sara Bay
with Tommy Armour, a transplanted Scot and the club's first golf professional. The two of them played formal exhibition matches against
pairs of the best pros in the country and also many friendly games.

In his book *Down the Fairway,* Jones admits to getting a lesson from
Armour and assistant Jimmy Donaldson, also of Sara Bay. "They told
me I was using too much right hand in the stroke," said Jones. "Whenever I could get the feel that I was pulling the club down and through
the stroke with the left arm it seemed impossible to get much off line."

Jones's comments make perfect sense because Armour believed the
left hand should lead the swing, and the right hand provided the power.

The characteristics of the Ross-designed Sara Bay course, namely tree-lined fairways (top), sloping greens (middle), and tightly manicured collection areas around the green (bottom), helped Jones hone a creative shot-making game.

Having said this, Armour's secret was footwork, as he points out in his best-selling book, *How to Play Your Best Golf All the Time*. According to Armour, when the golfer feels the pull of the left arm in the hitting area, it is an effect, not a cause. It is actually the shift of weight to the left foot and leg that triggers the downward pull sensation of the left arm and club.

When you consider that Jones had maybe the greatest footwork of all golfers, it's obvious that he learned the secret from Armour while they played Sara Bay.

Tree-lined fairways, a typical characteristic of the East Lake, Sara Bay, Pinehurst, and Seminole layouts designed by Ross—the dean of American course architects—require the golfer to make precision off the tee a bigger priority than power. Moreover, his trademark elevated greens, featuring slopes and crowns, reward pinpoint approach shots and run errant shots into collection areas or bunkers bordering the green. The secret to "going low" on a Ross course is to hit the ball to the part of the green that leaves you a fairly level putt.

Playing Ross-designed courses encouraged Jones to develop a controlled driving game. It also forced him to make distance control a priority on iron shots into the green, and to hone a polished short game that was necessary when finding the ball in one of those treacherous collection areas and facing a short pitch, delicate chip, or curving putt. This early education prepared Jones for the links courses of Scotland, on which the British Open and the British Amateur were played, and the extremely difficult courses that hosted the U.S. Open and the U.S. Amateur.

What You Can Learn from Bobby Jones

◆ Starting to play golf at a young age is a great advantage, particularly if you have supporting parents and friends you can compete against.

◆ Beginning the game with a limited number of clubs forces you to use your imagination and more quickly evolve into an inventive shot-maker.

◆ Modeling your swing technique after a talented golf professional's, as Jones did, can help you improve at a faster rate.

◆ The more courses you play, preferably in different areas of the country, the better, because you will be forced to learn how to hit a variety of shots out of a variety of lies.

2 NATURAL SELECTION

*Jones's unorthodox address led him to employ a
natural-flowing, powerful swing*

Like his model Stewart Maiden, Jones played
according to a set of fundamentals. However,
these basics, involving the grip, stance, body
alignment and clubface aim, were subtly different in most
cases and very different in others from the American
model. The reason was, Maiden had played golf in Scotland, where it is essential to hit the ball low under the
wind, so he set up different from American golf professionals, who preferred to hit the high fade shot. Maiden
was accustomed to playing the links course of Car-
noustie, where cold weather is common, so he was also
trained to play according to the hit-quick-and-walk philosophy. For this reason, Jones was encouraged not to dil-
lydally over the ball. After sizing up his target, he stepped
into the shot in a natural way, made a loose, relaxed
swing, and hit powerfully through the ball.

In Scotland, too, golf was regarded solely as sport.
Golfers went round the course in three hours, stopped at
the nineteenth hole for a whiskey, and went to work or

home to their family. Although things have changed somewhat over the last two decades, golf is still treated as pure sport overseas. Players don't get overly wrapped up in technique, as they do in America, unless the philosophy of the teacher is simple. Jones was lucky in this respect, because Maiden obviously shunned complex swing maxims, knowing they only confuse players, breed tension in the body, and thereby cause a faulty swing action and off-line shots. Maiden's simple philosophy—to swing the golf club up and around the body, down and out toward the ball, and through toward the target with the hands—was obviously right up Jones's alley since he, like most young boys, was impatient. Jones was a curious boy and also an avid reader. Had he not met Maiden, he would probably have been confused by the sundry and complex swing theories that appeared in books such as *Golf in America: A Practical Manual* (1895) by James Lee, *How to Play Golf* (1897) by H. J. Whigham, and *The Complete Golfer* (1908) by Harry Vardon.

Just by watching Jones set up and swing, onlookers could conclude that his preparation at address and his back and through motions were dictated by instinct and not by memorized mechanics. When he prepared for a wood or iron shot, his only intention was to hit the ball to the target using a natural-flowing swing. There were few steps to Jones's swing, no unnecessary thoughts of moving the club through certain points as if connecting dots on a page. The reason: he found out for himself, through trial and error, that thinking too much about specific swing positions, particularly on the downswing, caused him to hit bad shots. Other great players, most notably Jack Nicklaus and Severiano Ballesteros, agree. These two golfing legends believe the downswing is too instinctual and complex to be consciously directed.

By watching Maiden play, Jones learned the following: if you employ a good grip, set up to the ball comfortably and correctly with good posture, waggle the club back and forth a couple of times, use a forward press action of the hands to make a smooth transition into the backswing, and make a rhythmic hip-shift on the downswing, you give yourself the best possible chance of swinging the club on the proper path and plane virtually automatically and hitting the ball squarely and solidly.

Let's now look at the fundamentals, both classic and unorthodox, of the setup or address that Jones stuck to because they worked so well for Maiden and felt natural.

THE GRIP

Jones realized the hands are the only connection to the club and thus have the power to direct the clubface into the ball at impact, so he considered the grip the transmission of the golf swing.

Although Jones first used the interlock grip, when he turned eight he adopted the overlap grip originally popularized by Harry Vardon and employed by the majority of current PGA Tour, Senior PGA Tour, and LPGA Tour players. However, Jones failed to mention something in any of his instructional writings. Rather than resting his right pinky atop his left forefinger as Vardon recommended, Jones inserted it snugly between the left forefinger and left index finger. I feel, as Jones probably did, that this provides an added sense of comfort and ensures that the hands work as allies rather than adversaries. It is best that you experiment on the practice tee using both versions of the overlap grip to see if you like the Jones or Vardon method of holding the club.

Like Vardon and other great swingers of the club, Jones believed that the club should rest mainly in the fingers of both hands. The thumbs should rest down the sides of the shaft, and the overall pressure in the hands should be light enough to promote good clubhead feel. However, based on my analysis of Jones, I discovered that in other aspects of the grip he was indeed a rebel.

To enhance his control of the clubhead, Jones pressed a substantial portion of his right thumb against the top area of his right forefinger, rather than leaving a gap between the fingers. This was a secret he brushed over but one that you will discover makes a big difference to

One grip secret that Jones failed to share with golfers through his writings was pressing a substantial portion of his right thumb against the top area of his right forefinger. This position helps you control the clubhead during the swing.

your shot-making prowess. Jim Flick, a teacher I highly respect and the author of *Jim Flick on Golf*, explains why:

"You want the hands to function in harmony throughout the swing, so you can't afford any gaps that might contribute to breakdown. You wouldn't move your furniture cross-country in the back of a van if it were thrown in there loose, would you? If your hands come apart at the top of the backswing, it will be nigh impossible to keep the club on plane and under control during the forward swing."

Savvy enough to know that it's best and more natural to let the right hand provide the power in the swing, Jones also held the club more lightly in the right hand than in his left, which he considered the control hand. Furthermore, rather than set both hands on the club in a neutral position, as was commonly recommended by Jones himself, he, in fact, held the club with quite a strong left-hand grip and a weak right-hand. Whether he confused feel from fact, chose not to share another secret, or simply made an error in his writings does not really matter all that much. What matters is that, by turning his left hand clockwise a notch, he was poised to swing the club on a desired flat path needed to hit a draw. By setting his right hand on top of the club, with the *V* formed by the thumb and forefinger pointing up at his chin, it was preset essentially in the impact position, thereby increasing the odds of his returning there when the ball was struck with the clubface.

Before leaving the subject of the grip, I want to come back to a point made earlier about Jones pressing the right thumb against the right forefinger. My reason for returning is to show you first how fascinating the subject of instruction is, and second, to prove to you how grip technique varies according to the shot you want to hit.

I said earlier that one reason Jones pressed his right thumb against his right forefinger was to enhance his control over the clubface. More specifically, this position of the fingers allowed him to turn the clubface over slightly at impact, with the toe of the club leading the heel, in order to impart right-to-left draw-spin on the ball.

In sharp contrast, Ben Hogan's natural shot, the one he felt most comfortable playing, was a left-to-right fade. He wanted the clubface to finish slightly open at impact, so in gripping the club he took precautionary measures to prevent the right hand and arm from closing the clubface.

Hogan believed the right forefinger and the right thumb are great for opening doors and picking up coffee cups, but if you work these "pincer fingers" together and apply pressure, you will activate the muscles of the right arm and shoulder and hit a right-to-left shot. Therefore, he left a slight gap between the two fingers already referred to.

With respect to Hogan, I have never used my right thumb and forefinger to open a door or pick up a coffee cup, and I suspect neither did Jones. Moreover, Jones wanted to activate the right arm and shoulder in the hitting area, to add thrust to the swing, help him extend the club through the ball, and hit a powerful right-to-left draw shot. So he pressed his pincer fingers together fairly firmly.

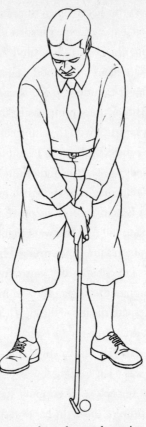

Jones believed that the setup, to a large degree, determines the type of swing employed by a player. Therefore, he was careful to bend comfortably and correctly at the knees and ball-and-socket joints of the hips.

POSTURE

Just like the pros he played with in tournaments, Jones flexed his knees slightly at address, bent over from the ball-and-socket joints of the hips, and stood comfortably erect with his body weight balanced on the ball of each foot. To help you match these vital starting positions, Georgia-based golf instructor Don Trahan believes you should lean forward, out and over the ball, as if preparing to make a dive from the edge of a pool.

When you set up like Jones, you create approximately a thirty-degree angle between the legs and spine. "This posture ensures that you stand the right distance from the ball and enables the body to turn more freely going back and coming down into the ball," says Mike Dunaway, former World Long Driving champion. "Further, it creates the proper angle at address at which ninety-five percent of all the work in the golf swing is done."

As to the positioning of the head, Jones advocated a chin-back concept. When you point the chin away from the target just slightly at address, keeping it a few inches away from the chest, you open up a clear passageway for the left shoulder to turn under it on the backswing and the right shoulder to turn under it on the downswing.

Although Jones recommended that the arms hang almost straight down from the shoulders and gave readers of his books the impression that his arms were stiff, he actually set up with what Jim McLean, one of *Golf Digest* magazine's top teachers in America, calls "spaghetti arms." Both arms were bent at the elbow, the left more than the right, since this position helped Jones employ a powerful lag swing.

Setting his hands a few inches behind the ball, also unorthodox, allowed Jones to push his hands back before the club. When you start back this way, then flick the club upward while cocking the wrists freely, you set yourself in position to unleash the hands and snap the club into the ball using a cock-recock action similar to that used by a cowboy to crack a whip. Ironically, neither Jones nor Hogan, who also set up with the hands behind the ball, ever mentioned this secret in their writings.

Just in case you think the hands-behind-ball position is quirky, listen to what former U.S. Open winner and CBS golf analyst Ken Venturi told me:

"I know that many teachers tell students to set up with their hands ahead of the ball when hitting a driver because it presets the hands in the impact position. But, the fact is the hands-ahead address can cause an overly steep backswing plane. I'd rather see a player start with the hands slightly behind the ball, since this position encourages a solid upswing hit—just what you want!"

STANCE

In speaking about the stance in his book *Bobby Jones on Golf*, Jones calls for the feet to be spread twelve inches apart. He also recommends that the golfer turn the left toe slightly outward and set the right foot exactly straight to the front, so it is perpendicular to the line of play. Surprisingly, in his book *The Basic Golf Swing*, Jones calls for both feet to be turned out. Let me clear things up.

My analysis of Jones is that he is a chameleon. When hitting long clubs, he stood to the ball using a one-foot-wide stance. However, in playing medium irons his stance got narrower, and narrower still when playing short irons, pitch and chip shots. My evidence also clearly shows that although Jones pointed his left foot outward, he did not always set his right foot at a right angle to the target line. When playing woods, long irons, and medium irons, he splayed his right foot outward, just as he did as he walked. This was indeed a swing secret he also failed to share with golfers, and one that encourages a free hip turn and flat swing.

"If your right foot splays out when you walk and you try to set it square to the target line when you set up to swing, it might offer resist-

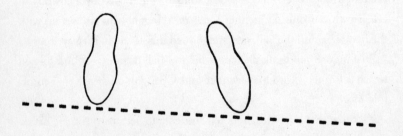

In setting up to play shots, Jones alternated between a closed stance (left) and open stance (right).

ance on the backswing, tense the lower right side, and promote a tendency to hit from the top," said Carl Lohren, one of *GOLF Magazine*'s top one hundred teachers in America and author of *One Move to Better Golf.*

When playing chips, Jones pointed the right foot left of the target line.

Only when playing short irons did he set the right foot down the way he said he did: perpendicular to the target line. This position restricts hip turn and promotes a compact upright swing, so its ideal for hitting controlled short irons requiring far less power than a driver. It also prevents an overly flat swing and hook shot, which is why Hogan used it when playing long and short clubs.

Something else that Jones did was change from a closed stance to an open stance when switching from his normal draw shot to a fade. The more he wanted to draw the ball, the more he'd drop his right foot back into a *closed* position. The more Jones wanted the ball to fade, the farther left or *open* he would set his feet in relation to the target line.

Jones felt more comfortable working the ball around the course. He favored a draw when playing a hole with a curve left or *dogleg,* when hitting a shot into a stiff wind, or when hitting an approach to a pin tucked behind a hazard on the left corner of the green. When the hole curved right, when the pin was located behind a hazard on the right side of the green, or when the green was firm, he hit a fade. Only when hitting a dead straight shot, say through a narrow opening in trees, would he set up with his feet parallel or *square* to the target line.

BALL POSITION

Jones believed ball position to be one of the most vital considerations of the setup, and one of the most personal.

When hitting standard full shots with the driver and fairway woods, he positioned the ball opposite his left instep. But as the clubs got shorter in length and more lofted, he moved the ball farther back in the

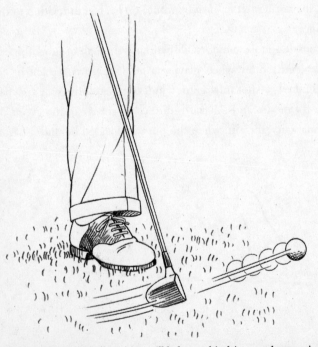

Copying Jones's forward ball position will help you hit drives on the upswing (left) and sweep the ball cleanly off the turf with irons (right).

stance. However, in playing any full shot he always played the ball forward enough to ensure a clean sweeping action.

When hitting chips, he normally played the ball opposite his right toe, but on these shots he was doing something entirely different: hitting down using a relatively sharp hit-and-hold action.

Jones felt strongly that there is one position for playing a shot with a particular club that enables you to hit the ball most easily and most efficiently. Yet he offered no suggestions other than those relative to correcting directional faults. His advice was to move the ball nearer the left foot to correct a slice and nearer the right foot to correct a hook.

Jack Nicklaus and two-time British Open winner Greg Norman believe that the ball should be positioned off the left heel for almost all shots. Arnold Palmer, however, believes the ball should move farther back in the stance as the clubs get shorter. Severiano Ballesteros, one of the most versatile shot-makers, has an entirely different opinion. He suggests that the ball be moved farther back of its normal position on days when you feel flexible and swing faster. On days when your body and the club move more slowly than on others, he believes you should position the ball farther forward to give your sluggish body more time to square up the clubface at impact. Jim McLean agrees with Ballesteros's flexible approach:

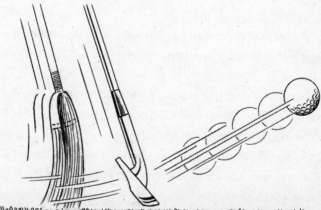

Here, the ball is positioned farther back than where Jones played it, but according to teacher Jim McLean, it still lies within the Corridors of Success. Jones would have approved, since he believed you should search for your own personal ball positions.

"Rather than recommending one setup or swing method, I believe in Corridors of Success—parameters within which I like to see any technique fall."

If you think your shot-making problems are caused by a fault in ball position, follow the advice of renowned British golf teacher John Jacobs. He recommends that you swing every club in the bag, except the putter, and determine where the clubhead contacts the grass. These spots—opposite the left heel, midway between the feet, etc.—should be your ball positions.

AIM

According to golf legend Sam Snead, when Jones set up to hit a straight shot, he played the ball off the toe of the club, knowing that, during the downswing, the arms extend to some degree, moving the club farther away from you. This stretching automatically brings the center of the

Jones's good setup was one chief reason why the club nearly always pointed directly at the target when he swung into the follow-through and his shots flew so accurately toward the target.

clubface directly into the ball and lets you follow through with the club pointing directly at the target.

Although Jones could curve the ball left or right, he did not do what some shot-makers do. He did not aim the clubface right when setting up to hit a draw and exaggerate the release of the clubface through impact. He did not aim the clubface left of the target when setting up to fade and delay the release by holding on firmly with the left hand.

I think Jones's way of shaping shots is intelligent because it requires less practice, clubhead feel, and timing. Essentially, all you do is aim the body in the direction the ball will start flying on, and the club at your final target. After that, just swing normally.

What You Can Learn from Bobby Jones

◆ For best results, minimize your swing thoughts ("keys").

◆ When gripping the club, let your right pinky rest snugly between your left forefinger and left index finger, and press your right thumb fairly firmly against your right forefinger.

◆ Pointing your right foot outward slightly, especially when playing the long clubs, will promote a strong body turn and powerful shot.

◆ When driving, position the ball opposite your left heel to promote an upswing hit.

◆ Move the ball back slightly in your stance as the clubs get shorter.

◆ When playing a straight shot, position the ball closer to the toe of the club than its heel.

3 SWING SAVVY

Jones's secrets to perfectly coordinating the movement of the body with the movement of the golf club

It's certainly an exaggeration for me to call Jones's graceful, perfectly timed swing the Eighth Wonder of the World. However, there is no doubting that his action was natural and unstrained, with the backswing flowing ever so smoothly into the downswing action. "There could be no more fascinating player to watch for the free and rhythmic character of the swing," wrote Bernard Darwin, the famous English golf-scribe, in the book *Golf Between Two Wars*.

Jones's natural swing contrasted sharply with the highly mechanical swings of his fellow amateurs and also those employed by the professionals he competed against at home and abroad. For this reason, Jones's swing can be called *classic* in the true sense of the word. And he built it essentially by trusting his instincts to create a swing that fit him and a swing he was able to ingrain and repeat, which is precisely the advice the late golf teacher Davis Love Jr. gave to students.

From 1916 to 1930, Jones won twenty-three of the

Bobby Jones, the smoothest swinger of all time, in action.

fifty-two tournaments he entered, and thirteen of twenty-seven major championships. Assessing Jones's phenomenal record and low scoring average, earned by hitting such a high percentage of good shots and so few bad shots, it's not surprising that he is still considered by some noted golf experts to be the best player ever. About as consistent as a baseball player who bats .900, Jones was truly in a league all his own, although, admittedly, Tiger Woods is fast making his mark on the golf world.

What was most responsible for Jones's success, more than a strong heart and mind, feel for distance, and touch around the greens, was the efficiency of his swing. Jones's swing flowed as smoothly and rhythmically as a piece of music by Chopin, and he gradually built up speed, controlled speed, until the final crescendo of impact, when the ball exploded off the clubface. His swing was so rhythmic that I wonder if he had studied anatomy and combined his knowledge of how the feet, knees, hips, shoulders, arms, and hands must work with what he learned about physics and engineering at Georgia Tech University. Jones knew the ins and outs—the secrets—to good golf technique, and through his own experimentation, in practice and in play, together with the insights into the swing he learned from Maiden, he was able to break the code and solve the mystery of the swing. Jones had golf technique down to a science. That Jones's swing operated effortlessly and flowed smoothly from one stage to another, much like dominoes falling over, proved that each and every part of his body stuck to its individual job description, orchestrated by Jones. Jones made sure that each job was done and done right—from pushing off the left foot to trigger the backswing, to winding up the body to create power, to replanting the left heel and shifting the hips to set the downswing in motion, to unhinging the wrists and driving the club through the ball with maximum controlled acceleration.

What is so fascinating about Jones's swing is that it matches up with the technological advancements in club design. Jones played with hickory shafts similar, at least in flexibility, to the soft steel and graphite shafts of today.

"These shafts continue to increase in popularity because they are lighter, help you to get a better sense of where the weighted clubhead is during the swing, allow you to generate high clubhead speed in the impact zone, and gain as much as twenty yards in distance," said Nick Mastroni, former equipment writer for *GOLF* and *Golf Illustrated* magazines.

JONES'S MASTERFUL TECHNIQUE:
THE BACKSWING

That Jones once tried to convince former tour professional Cary Middlecoff to start the backswing on a certain count gives us insight into Jones's secret to an extrasmooth swing. Middlecoff, who played with Jones, observed that Jones began his swing by means of a rhythmic pattern involving a count.

"Jones would plant first the right foot and then the left, combine a slight forward press with a single waggle of the club, and go quickly yet smoothly into the backswing," said Middlecoff in his book *The Golf Swing*. "It seemed to go on a count of one, two, three, swing."

What Middlecoff did not mention was that Jones pushed off his left foot to trigger the swing. This is a good triggering device, provided you let weight roll across the left foot until it rests on the inside of the ball of the big toe and, practically simultaneously, move the left knee outward to promote a body coil and not a sway to the right.

The sway is basically an exaggerated side-to-side lateral movement away from the target. Surprisingly, a faulty sway is the result of an honest effort by the player to shift the weight correctly over to the right foot and leg on the backswing, so he or she can return the weight to the left side on the downswing and hit with power. All the same, understand what Jones understood: swaying the upper body straight back away from the target is a deadly error, because barring some kind of contorted compensatory movement, you will not be able to sway

A gentle push off the left foot helped Jones swing the club back smoothly.

To promote a rounded swing and more powerful turning action of the body, set your right foot down Jones style (left), not Hogan style (right).

back to exactly the same position from which you started. Consequently, it's inevitable that you will mistime the swing and mishit the shot.

Since the earliest golf instruction books were written, thousands and thousands of words have been devoted to the mechanics of the weight shift. However, Jones discovered that the shift happens automatically when you turn the hips clockwise on the backswing.

Jones also learned that if he coiled the shoulders fully, the club would swing nicely inside and behind the body virtually automatically. This must have brought him great relief, because players and teachers of his era believed you should consciously pull the club back along an inside path to prevent an outside take-away and ultimately a slice.

Now is a good time to bring up a technical point relayed to students by more and more teachers across the country. Many coaches are instructing students to "swing the club in front of the body" when playing full shots. Please excuse me for being so frank, but Jones must be turning over in his grave since he was a strong advocate of a rounded action and swinging the club back inside the target line. My advice is to ignore this coaches' tip or else you will swing on too steep a plane, chop down on the ball, and hit slice shots off the tee and fat iron shots into the green. Try to emulate Jones's flat action by swinging more around the body and through the ball rather than straight up and down. Setting up like Jones, with the right foot turned out to play woods and irons, as opposed to pointing it directly at the target line, Hogan style, will help promote a more active hip turn and rounded swing.

"I have always favored a method that brings the club back well away from the line of play—around the body, if you please—because such a stroke has the advantage of greater power without sacrificing accuracy," said Jones in *Bobby Jones on Golf*.

To show how ahead of his time Jones was, here is what teacher Butch Harmon told me when we worked on the book *The Four Cornerstones of Winning Golf*:

"For the driver to be moving through impact at a shallow angle, the entire swing must be on a relatively flat plane, a little more around the body than up and down. A good way to accomplish this—after the initial take-away move of your arms-shoulders triangle—is by swinging your left forearm more across your chest than upward. I don't agree with teachers who tell students to reach for the sky on the backswing. This creates separation of the arms from the body rather than having the body and arms swing as a unit. And it definitely creates too steep an angle of attack on the downswing, particularly for the driver. I might add that Greg Norman, whose swing was upright in the 1980s, has flattened his swing plane with the driver and gained great accuracy to go with his distance."

Jones also believed that flatness of the swing results from a correct body turn and not from manipulation of the club by the hands and wrists. When you try to keep the club in front of the body, the tendency is to lift the club straight up into the air on an overly steep plane. Again, from that steep at-the-top position, you can do little else but chop down on the ball at impact. When driving, hitting fairway woods, and long irons, you want to sweep the club through impact. The only way to accomplish this goal is to let the club swing back low and along an inside path once the hips and shoulders begin coiling in a clockwise direction.

In swinging the club back, Jones was strict about order. *The body must move first, the arms second, the clubhead last*. He was also careful not to jerk the club back with the hands even though they are the only connection to the club. In the initial stages of the swing, when the club first travels back low along the target line, then inside it due to the turning action of the shoulders, you must feel as if the hands are only going along for a ride as the left arm extends. As the world's number one teacher, David Leadbetter, says, "At this early stage in the swing, your hands are passive and only move in response to your body."

The hands should feel dead until your left heel lifts off the ground as Jones's did, weight shifts to the instep of your right foot, and your wrists feel as if they want to hinge due to the swinging weight of the clubhead. Jones let his wrists hinge quite early in the backswing, which was extraordinary. However, he certainly knew what he was doing. This early set action, adopted in later years by golfing great Johnny Miller, who called it "more natural," allows you to make a full and tension-free backswing and be poised to employ a late release on the downswing to create power.

"Supple wrists are unquestionably to be desired in playing golf," wrote Jones in *Bobby Jones on Golf*. "Stiff wrists destroy timing, rhythm, and every hope of control. It is a condition which places the direct control of the club in the shoulders and body of the player."

How do you promote play in the wrists? By gripping the club lightly, like Jones.

If you choose to adopt the Jones method, once the wrists fully hinge, you must also let the right knee straighten to allow the right hip to turn freely and fully and thereby provide the thrust necessary for pushing the club to the top. To strengthen the turn and increase your power quotient, concentrate on keeping weight on the inside of your right foot. If you let weight move to the outside of your right foot, you will weaken your body coil and thus drain vital power from the swing.

One vital link to swinging the club back on the correct path and plane is to continue coiling your body while keeping your right elbow fairly close to your side, and your left wrist *flat* (in line with the left forearm). Any indentation in the area between the left forearm and the back of the left wrist usually signals an overly upright swing and open clubface position. A flat left-wrist position ensures that the clubface is square. This means you'll be more likely to return the clubface squarely to the ball at impact without manipulating the handle with your hands.

Having worked with a number of tour pros and top teachers, on books and magazine articles, one of the hottest subjects during the 1990s was the length of the backswing. There was a trend to shorten the swing, but in the new millennium, top golfers, most notably Tiger Woods, have returned to a longer swing. Granted, the typical tour player does not swing the club back quite so far as Jones did, or John Daly does today. Nevertheless, the average swing is longer now with the clubshaft passing the parallel position—the point at the top when the clubshaft parallels the target line.

Jones believed the golfer should swing the club well past parallel with the clubhead pointing slightly right of target, or *across the line* as teach-

As you swing the club up like Jones, let your right knee straighten, so it becomes a solid post for your hips to pivot around.

ers refer to this position. In fact, in *The Basic Golf Swing,* he wrote, "A great many more shots are spoiled by a swing that is too short than by one that is too long." Fred Couples, one of the PGA Tour's power hitters, agrees, citing several advantages to the long backswing, including:

1. It creates a bigger arc and gives you more time to build acceleration.

2. It encourages a stronger stretch of the body and thus more stored energy available to increase the power of the downswing.

3. It makes it easy to start down from inside the target line, which helps you deliver the club squarely into the ball and hit it accurately.

4. It gives you additional time to create clubhead speed and prepare to unleash power at the moment of impact.

In the modern era, the swings of players Payne Stewart and John Daly come closest to resembling Jones's action. Both players, by virtue of their success in major championships, prove the worth of Jones's swing.

The late Payne Stewart, who died tragically in a plane crash, used his feet so wonderfully, rolling onto his right foot during the backswing and the left foot during the downswing, you'd think he was Fred Astaire. Like Jones, he also kept his left arm tension-free once his wrists hinged on the backswing. When reaching the top, his body was coiled to the maximum, readied to unleash the club solidly into the ball, and the club crossed the line. At the start of the downswing, Stewart's right elbow dropped down close to the body while the club fell into the ideal hitting position.

Daly, like Jones, makes a long backswing and points the clubhead just right of target at the top, proving that he swung the club back and did not lift it straight into the air, which is a common fault of amateurs. Regardless of Daly's off-and-on problems, on the course he is a powerful driver and world-class player, as evidenced by his two major wins:

the 1991 PGA and the 1995 British Open. I had the great pleasure of working with Daly on the book *Grip It and Rip It!* and I can tell you that he proves Jones's swing theories are correct. In talking to Daly, he cleared up a few issues regarding the extralong cross-the-line swing that Jones failed to talk about even though it was quite obviously another of his most vital swing secrets. I'd like to share what I learned so you can play better golf and stand up to the critics when they tell you that it's the wrong technique.

At the top of your backswing, the clubshaft is on line if it points exactly parallel to the target line. Generally, this is considered the most desired position to be in under the premise that there's no need to manipulate the club on the downswing to produce a square hit.

If the clubshaft points to the left of the target at the top, you'd be in a *laid-off* position. Not too many teachers favor this position because when the clubshaft is pointing to the left of the target, it means that your hands are somewhat closer to the target line than you'd like them to be, and the clubhead's farther away from it (more to the left). From this position, it's easy for the right shoulder and your hands to come over the ball from outside in. These swing faults usually cause the average golfer to slice and the better golfer to hit a pull or a pull-hook. However, the results are never carved in stone. Ben Hogan played from a slightly laid-off position and hit the ball awfully well.

Now, if the clubshaft crosses or points to the right of the target at the top, you are considered to be *crossing the line*. It's been argued that the path of the club on the downswing will tend to mirror the line the clubshaft is pointing to at the top, so if anything, you are likely to swing through the ball from inside out. This starts the ball to the right of the target line and usually imparts a right-to-left spin on the ball so that a draw or a hook will result.

If you look at the top-of-swing positions of today's PGA Tour professionals from behind, you'll notice that the majority of them cross the line. This is not too surprising, when you consider that this position is just a natural result of trying to make a big body coil and a long Jones-like backswing. Furthermore, since in a Jones-type swing the arms swing on a more upright plane than the shoulders, you are more likely to cross the line at the top and hit a draw shot.

In swinging the club all the way back like Jones, let the turning action of your body be free and full. It's truly a technical must that you increase your shoulder turn if you are going to increase power in your swing. Just knowing that you should turn as far as possible, while maintaining good balance throughout the backswing, should help you employ a stronger coil. However, if your muscles, particularly those in your back and shoulders, feel stiff, purchase a heavy-weighted club from your local golf professional and practice swinging it a few times per day.

As you continue turning your shoulders up to the fullest coil, remember to keep turning your hips as far as possible, in the same clockwise manner. Some pros teach a theory of resistance by the hips—that is, minimizing hip turn and maximizing shoulder turn. The idea is that you build up tremendous torque between the upper and lower body right at the waist, which you will then automatically unleash into a powerful downswing action. Ben Hogan believed this to be true. Bobby Jones disagreed, arguing that trying to coil one part of the body fully while resisting with another is too darn complicated for the average golfer to coordinate successfully. Like Daly today, Jones believed that you should turn the hips and shoulders as far as is comfortably possible since a full body turn ultimately unleashes a more powerful downswing release than the resisting-hips backswing does.

When Jones reached the top, his shoulders were coiled one hundred degrees, his hips around sixty degrees—more than even he believed. To improve your golf, try to match these positions and be sure:

1. Your left heel lifts off the ground.

"The only way to achieve a full weight shift and promote a rhythmic swing is to allow your left heel to lift off the ground," says David Lee, one of *GOLF Magazine*'s top one hundred teachers in America.

2. Your back faces the target and there are "serious" wrinkles in your shirt.

"Trying to match this position of Jones's helps you balance weight

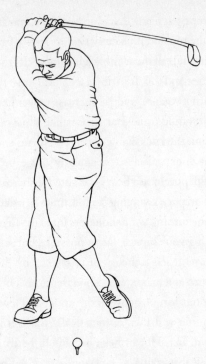

Jones's past-parallel, cross-the-line swing was ahead of its time. More and more PGA Tour and LPGA Tour pros are now employing long swings. You should, too, because this action is more natural and powerful.

correctly on your right foot and coil your body powerfully," says John Anselmo, Tiger Woods's former teacher.

3. Your right hip pocket is behind you. In other words, when looking at a front-view photograph showing you in the at-the-top swing position, the right hip pocket would not be visible.

"Rotating your right hip fully clockwise helps you make a stronger shoulder turn and is thus a major power move," says teaching guru Gerald McCullagh.

4. Your upper body weight is on your left side, your lower body weight on your right side.

"This is the ultimate way to achieve balance in the swing," says Ken Butler of the United States Golf Teachers Federation.

5. Your left knee points more outward than inward.

"This helps ensure a stable foundation to swing from," says John Gerring, who is one of America's most respected golf instructors.

6. Your left shoulder blade is behind the ball.

"Striving for this position prevents a reverse pivot fault and ensures strong shots," says supercoach Jim McLean of the Doral Resort and Country Club in Miami, Florida.

7. Your left arm is extended but not stiff.

"Letting your left arm extend in a tension-free manner is far more natural than trying to keep it stiff," says Charles Sorrell, one of *GOLF Magazine*'s top one hundred teachers in America. "In turn, this relaxed position allows powerful energy to flow through the arm and be transmitted to the golf club at impact."

8. Your right elbow is relatively close to your body and pointing down at the ground.

"Arriving in this position is the only consistent way to swing the club on the proper plane, just like the great Bobby Jones did," says Missouri-based teacher Rick Grayson.

9. Your right wrist is hinged slightly.

"Being in this relaxed position enhances your feel for the clubhead and thus makes you poised to return the clubface squarely to the ball," says Rick Whitfield, golf director at the prestigious Loblolly Pines Golf Club in Hobe Sound, Florida, and one of the best teachers in the United States.

JONES'S MASTERFUL TECHNIQUE: THE DOWNSWING

Jones disagreed with those golfers of his day who believed the downswing is purely an automatic response to a good backswing. He felt that a subtle movement of the hips was the best way to ensure a smooth transition from the top into impact, then through the ball. What Jones failed to share was an important secret that helped him make a lateral hip-shift: replanting the ball of the left foot on the turf first. In turn, this mini-shift causes the right arm and elbow to return close to the body and gives the upper body and club time to play catch-up with the lower body.

When watching footage of Jones swinging, I'm reminded of what teacher Rick Smith said to me when we worked together on the book *How to Find Your Perfect Golf Swing*. Smith, best known for teaching tour players Phil Mickelson and Lee Janzen, said, "In making the transition into the downswing, the left hip moves laterally first, which moves weight to the forward leg, then moves more rotationally as the body and arms move to impact and beyond.

"Even though we can segregate and examine arm motion and body

Jones's lateral hip-shift allows the right arm, right elbow, and club to drop into the hitting slot.

motion in the swing separately, there is a strong relation between the two. The better your arms swing, the better your body motion tends to be. The better your body motion, the better your arm swing tends to be."

As the hands, arms, and club drop downward, albeit on a flatter plane than the backswing, it's important that you not fall victim to the hit impulse and pull the club down into the ball, with the wrists unhinging. This early release will surely lead to a mishit shot, so trust the club to be returned to the ball by virtue of all the good things done previously.

"Any attempt to hit at the ball with your right shoulder, arm, and/or hand will throw the club outside the plane you swing the club on, and also outside the target line," says Phil Ritson, a former mentor of renowned teacher David Leadbetter. "This damaging over-the-top move also causes the clubhead to come into the impact zone at an undesirable steep angle. The end result of early right-side domination for most amateurs is a dreaded slice."

Since the club swings back on the inside, it's necessary that you rotate your left hip to the left of target, *clear* it, once you feel weight shift to your left foot and leg. This one move opens up a passageway for the clubface to head toward the ball instead of pointing right of target.

The moment you clear the left hip, the left leg should be allowed to straighten at the knee, so that it becomes a solid post to coil against.

As Jones turned around this solid left-leg post and his shoulders and hips continued to uncoil, it was obvious that like all good players he blanked out. Jones realized what all fine players know is true about the downswing motion: once centrifugal force takes over, the wrists start to unhinge and the right arm begins to straighten, and the club accelerates toward the ball. By just letting the downswing happen and allowing no conscious movement of the club with the hands, Jones was able to consistently bring the clubface solidly into the back of the ball at impact.

Although Jones's downswing operated, to a large degree, on automatic pilot, he was well aware that the left arm and hand play the lead

You'll accelerate the club into impact like Jones if you clear the left hip, rotate the right hip counterclockwise, and let centrifugal force take control.

role in guiding the club into impact, while the right arm and wrist provide the power. For the right side to create oomph in the hitting area, your right arm and right wrist must straighten. If these vital moves are not happening at the right time in your swing, follow the advice of golf instructor Peter Croker: "Concentrate on flailing or throwing the club at the ball." This dual action that Jones compared to the ones used in cracking a whip will help you increase clubhead velocity and allow you to hit the ball farther.

Because Jones swung into the ball from well inside the target line, with the club's toe slightly ahead of its heel through impact, he naturally imparted right-to-left overspin on the ball and hit a classic draw shot. The shot he hit flew low with overspin; thus the ball bored into the wind and was ideal when playing a shot around a hole that curves to the left.

The follow-through and the finish of the swing are more reactions to the backswing than premeditated acts. Still, you should check these key positions to see if you're swinging at the highest efficiency level:

1. In the follow-through, when the hands reach waist level, the back of your right hand should be parallel to the target line.

2. When swinging into the finish, you should feel that almost all your body weight is on the outside of your left foot and all but the very tip of your right shoe is off the ground. Also, your belly button should face slightly left of target since this position proves that you released your left side and made a free and fluid swing.

3. If you need any further confirmation, look at the ball flying down the fairway.

The advantage Jones had over other amateurs (and pros, too) was a far superior rhythmic swing, one that can be attributed to a smooth tempo and perfect timing. Jones's light right-hand grip allowed him to know, through feel, exactly where the club was at all times during the swing. Jones's left hand guided the club along the desired path. This special talent, combined with knowing exactly what his feet, knees, hips, hands, wrists, arms, and shoulders were doing from start to finish, allowed him to repeat a good swing over and over.

Sandy Lyle, former winner of the Masters and British Open championships, has a theory about the swing that applies to Jones's action. He thinks of the swing as a range of tones. If his tempo is "on song," the speed of his swing builds up steadily, just as the pitch of a singer's voice gets higher as he or she goes from do, to re, to me, to fa, to sol, to la, to te, to do. Lyle prefers this image to saying "One" as the club swings from the address to the top of the swing, and "Two" as the club swings from the top to impact. I agree. As Lyle told me, this gimmick, which is commonly taught, tends to hinder tempo. First of all, it sets up a pause at the top that is against the laws of swing technique. Second, it makes no sense, for the swing should not be thought of as two halves, and certainly not two equal halves. It should take you approxi-

You'll play better golf if you look like Jones in the follow-through (left) and early finish position (right).

mately one and a half seconds to swing the club from the address position to the top, and a mere fifth of a second to return the club from the top into impact. So, don't fall into the trap of believing that "one" equals "two." The swing beat is not split up into two equal parts of approximately one second each; it quickens as the club comes closer to hitting the ball.

Yet another reason why Jones swung the club so smoothly is that he allowed the head to rotate slightly, having realized early on that trying to keep the head still creates tension in the swing, and letting it move too much causes the body to sway.

Without question, one of the oldest tenets of golf instruction is that you must keep your head still throughout the golf swing. However, the swings of the best players exhibit free-flowing head movement in the

backswing, downswing, and follow-through. It's okay if you allow your head to rotate slightly if you discover this helps the rhythm of your backswing and downswing.

A little bit of head movement is better than trying to keep it locked in position. If you make keeping your head perfectly still your number one priority throughout the swing, you'll end up restricting your swing motion and fail to develop the necessary body rotation needed for long, straight shots. You'll end up hitting at the ball rather than swinging through it. Also, straining to keep your head rooted past impact can lead to neck strains and possibly more severe injuries.

On the downswing, remember the movement of your shoulders is somewhat of a seesaw action. The turning action of the shoulders through the downswing, perpendicular to your spine, brings the right shoulder down under the chin while the left shoulder works back up.

However, instead of forcing your head to stay down as the right shoulder moves past it, it's much better to let your head rotate slightly, swiveling along with your shoulders through the impact zone and into the follow-through. The result will be a much smoother move through the hitting area.

Jones's swing and magnificent control of the golf club allowed him to hit great shots that won him championships around the world. Let's now look at how he played four bread-and-butter shots.

What You Can Learn from Bobby Jones

◆ In swinging the club like Jones, it's a smart idea to use a flexible steel or graphite shaft.

◆ Swing the club around your body, on a natural, flat arc.

◆ In swinging the club back, let the body move first, the arms second, the club last.

◆ Let the wrists hinge freely on the backswing, so you're poised to make a powerful release of the club through impact.

◆ On drives, a long backswing and strong body coil is better than a short backswing and restricted turn.

◆ Let your left heel lift off the ground to encourage a free and full windup of the body.

◆ Replant your left heel during the downswing and your timing and ball-striking ability will improve.

◆ To promote accuracy, lead the club into the ball with your left hand.

◆ To create power in the impact zone, let the right arm and right wrist straighten.

4 SUPERSHOTS

Learning to play the supercontrolled power draw, supercontrolled power fade, wind-cheater, and high cut—the Bobby Jones way

Quite recently, I watched an absolutely spectacular made-for-television documentary on jazz done by Ken Burns. I stayed glued to my seat throughout the show and particularly loved the footage of Louis Armstrong. When Armstrong played the trumpet, he seemed to be a genius who could change the mood of the world just by pressing a little more lightly or firmly on the valves of the instrument or blowing harder or more softly into the mouthpiece.

Though Jones played golf and not music, he also was certainly a genius, whose creative shots from the tee or fairway brought goose bumps to members of the gallery. Jones was able to make the ball move in a particular direction, left or right, low or high, simply by making subtle changes to his body alignment or ball position, or by gripping the club just a little more firmly or lightly than normal.

The supershots that Jones played so wonderfully from the tee were the *supercontrolled power draw* and the *supercontrolled power fade.* When hitting an approach shot into the green from fairly far out, he often played a *wind-cheater,* which flew extralow, or a *high cut,* which sat down quickly upon landing.

Jones was a much more inventive and daring shot-maker than Hogan, who just about always played a fade for fear of duck-hooking the ball. When it came to shot-making, Jones was in a league all his own, particularly off the tee.

Jones realized that driving a golf ball a good distance down the fairway is as important to shooting low scores as scrambling around the green or sinking putts. Now if that sounds like too profound a statement in light of the old cliché "Drive for show, putt for dough," consider these points:

1. On a regulation eighteen-hole course, the majority of holes are par fours and par fives. Therefore, the driver or number one wood is the club most often used off the tee.

2. Many of today's golf architects design courses with narrow fairways and penal rough to counter state-of-the-art metal drivers that are more player-friendly and forgiving and hit the ball longer distances. Hence, it's more critical than ever before to keep tee shots on the short grass.

3. A good drive, especially on the opening hole, raises a player's confidence, and that faith in one's ability positively affects the rest of his or her game.

4. Well-hit, well-directed drives put a player in position to hit on-target approach shots that set up good scoring opportunities.

5. Because many par-four holes are around 400 yards and par fives average 500 yards, a player who hits accurate drives only around 220 yards can play low-handicap golf with just an adequate approach-shot game and short game.

6. The standard length of a driver is 43.5 inches. Being the longest club in the bag, it is the most awkward to swing. However, if a golfer learns how to swing a driver first, swinging the fairway woods and irons will be far easier.

As Jones discovered from watching Maiden, several vital steps to developing a first-class driving game do not involve the swing itself, but the preswing routine. Here's what you should do to prepare for hitting a creative tee shot.

So that you more carefully scrutinize the hole's shape and the hazards bordering the fairway, start your routine by standing a few paces behind the tee markers and look straight down the fairway. What you should be doing at this stage of your routine is picking out the ideal path for the ball to start flying along and also the premier area of fairway for it to land on. Here's an example to help you learn to plan out your shots:

Assume the hole you are about to play curves from right to left and the draw is your preferred shot. From your standing position behind the ball, try to see in your mind's eye a ball-flight path that starts down the right side of the fairway and curves to the left once it reaches its peak. If the hole curves in the opposite direction, visualize the ball fading toward its final target in the fairway.

Once you choose a shot and visualize a perfect result, you are ready to tee the ball up. Tee the ball close to the left marker on dogleg-left holes and close to the right marker on dogleg-right holes.

Let's now look into the advantages of playing creative golf shots and learn the most important setup and swing techniques involved.

SUPERCONTROLLED POWER DRAW

Whenever you play a par-four hole that curves dramatically left, the supercontrolled power-draw shot will help you cut the corner of the dogleg and hit the ball longer via added roll, so that you effectively shorten the hole.

Say the hole you're playing is 420 yards and curves left or doglegs at the 200-yard mark. Say also that when you hit a reasonably solid drive, you get about 240 yards on the shot.

In the situation just cited, your normal straight drive will land in the middle of the fairway. Nevertheless, because the hole turns to the left in the landing area, the ball will either finish up on the right side of the fairway or in light rough. Since the hole's length is measured along the center of the fairway, you're actually making the hole play longer, say 435 yards instead of 420. Therefore, your 240-yard drive may actually leave you 195 yards to the center of the green, probably a long iron with a tough angle to negotiate.

By hitting a winding draw in the style of Jones, you can bend the ball around the corner on a fly, with the right-to-left spin imparted on it making it finish in the left center of the fairway. This should allow you to cut 15 yards off the hole, making it play around 405 yards. Also, remember that because of its penetrating flight pattern and additional roll, you'll average about 20 extra yards by playing the big draw. Thus your second shot will end up being only 145 yards. That's 50 yards less than you'd have with a straight shot, plus you'll enjoy a much better angle to the flag on your approach shot, making it easier to hit the ball close to the hole and set up a birdie putt.

Another ideal situation for playing the supercontrolled power draw is when the hole is straight, and the right side of a wide fairway is of a right-to-left contour. Here, by landing the ball on the slope, so that it bounces off it and runs toward the middle of the fairway, you can pick up as much as 35 yards. Jones no doubt followed this strategy when playing the rolling links courses of Scotland when competing in the British Open and the British Amateur.

Ironically, Jones was smart to also use the supercontrolled power draw on narrow holes featuring a fairway sloping dramatically from left to right. From experience, he learned that the draw is a high-percentage shot that allows you to keep the ball in play. This is because the drawing action of the ball as it descends will make it counteract the left-to-right slope of the fairway, so it sits down rather quickly running along the slope. Jones discovered, as you will, that this is a useful shot when the fairway slopes toward a water hazard, a high-lipped fairway bunker, out of bounds, or deep rough. You'll give up perhaps 10 yards by drawing the ball into the slope, but on holes where keeping the ball in the fairway is extremely important, this shot-making strategy is the most intelligent.

Jones also used the supercontrolled power draw to battle windy conditions off the tee. In fact, his ability to master this shot allowed him to win many championships on days when the wind blew into his face. You'll almost always maximize your distance into the wind by playing this powerful shot. Since the shot will be hit with a clubface that's closed in relation to the path of the swing, the ball will shoot out in a lower than normal trajectory, so the wind will not affect it as much.

There are yet other advantages to playing the supercontrolled power draw. On long par-four holes, you'll pick up added yardage, particularly on fast-running fairways. So you will be able to come into the green with a shorter, more lofted club, which makes it easier to hit the shot close to the pin than with a long iron.

On par-five holes, the supercontrolled power draw will give you an added advantage, especially if the wind is blowing from the right. Average hitters will be able to set up a shorter third shot, and longer hitters can reach the green in two.

What follows is Jones's savvy setup and swing techniques for playing this shot.

To promote draw-spin, Jones teed up higher than normal so that the entire ball was just above the clubface. This tee trick, familiar only to the sharpest golfers, automatically promotes the flat swing path required for this shot. According to Senior PGA Tour pro Chi Chi Rodriguez, a shot-maker par excellence, "The flat arc of swing allows the hands and forearms to rotate over in a more exaggerated clockwise direction, causing the clubface to close slightly and impart right-to-left spin on the ball."

Rather than aim both the body and the club well right of target and use exaggerated hand action to shut the clubface, Jones aimed the clubface directly at his target, then aimed his feet, body, and his grip slightly

In setting up to play the supercontrolled power draw Jones's way, tee the ball higher than normal.

to the right of it. As a general rule, the more draw-spin you want to impart on the ball, the farther right you should aim the body. Do not ever align the clubface to the right of where you want the ball to finish. Anytime your clubface points off the line, you set yourself up to manipulate the club through impact in an attempt to return it to a position square to the target line.

Once you feel comfortable that you have copied Jones's setup, just make a normal swing and watch the ball fly from right to left in the air.

SUPERCONTROLLED POWER FADE

Various course situations prompted Jones to play a left-to-right fade shot rather than his more natural draw. For example, on a hole that curves or doglegs right, the object is to cut off some of the hole's distance and keep the ball on the fairway.

The fade shot is also ideal for extremely narrow par-four holes, since it's easier to control than the draw. This is because the fade does not roll as far after it lands. So whenever the fairway is a narrow landing strip bordered by rough, trees, or hazards, consider the supercontrolled power fade your shot-making choice. After all, it worked for Bobby en route to winning the 1930 U.S. Open at Minnesota's Interlachen Country Club course, featuring especially narrow fairways.

Whenever the driving area slopes right to left and there's trouble down the left side, the fade is also a good choice of shot. Its left-to-right spin will counteract the slope in the fairway, and while the ball will not run very far, it will finish in the fairway.

Jones realized that the fade carries a higher trajectory than either the draw or straight shot, so he also played it when the wind blew from left to right and he was looking to pick up extra yardage off the tee.

In hitting the fade, Jones teed up lower than normal, so the ball was just about even with the top of the clubface. This seemingly minor adjustment, plus setting your feet open (right foot closer to the target line than the left foot) will allow you to swing the club on a more upright plane. This plane of swing brings the clubhead into the ball on a slightly steeper angle. Further, the more upright plane is naturally more conducive to applying fade-spin on the ball.

Another adjustment Jones made was to weaken his left-hand grip slightly so it matched his weak right-hand grip. This grip also encourages an upright swing and automatically delays the release of the forearms and club through impact, forcing the clubface to arrive at impact slightly open.

Jones aimed the clubface directly at his target. Avoid trying to fade the ball by aiming the clubface to the left, then trying to manipulate it open through impact. This swing strategy is like playing the lottery. Inevitably, at times you won't open the face enough; other times you'll overdo it and hit a wild slice.

Another setup adjustment that Jones paid close attention to was ball

In setting up to play the supercontrolled power fade Jones's way, tee the ball lower than normal.

position. He played the ball slightly forward of its normal position for driving because this encouraged him to slide his hips laterally for a longer period and actually sort of block the ball out to the right.

Once Jones was satisfied that his revised setup was correct, he swung the club normally.

WIND-CHEATER SHOT

Many club-level players, perhaps you, feel extremely uncomfortable playing a fairway iron shot into a stiff wind. The main reason is, they are unaware of the basic fundamentals for hitting a low, piercing shot. Typically, the high-handicap player positions the ball well back in the stance, with the hands a few inches ahead of it. Because this address position promotes an overly steep swing, the player hits a shot that rises quickly high into the air—balloons—then drops virtually straight down, well short of the target. That the player swings faster than normal only magnifies the problem. He or she hits down so sharply and creates so much backspin that the ball flies higher still.

When competing in the 1930 British Open, played at Hoylake in England, Jones realized that a strong headwind magnifies errors in striking, so he concentrated on hitting the ball straighter and not harder. In fact, after setting up with his feet square to the target, the ball back only slightly, and the hands just slightly ahead of the ball, he swung the club

Striving for a short finish will encourage you to automatically chase the ball with the club through impact and hit a solid wind-cheating shot.

back inside the target line and at a slower pace than normal to enhance control.

On the downswing, Jones chased the ball with the clubhead for a longer period through impact, then employed a shorter finish. To help you swing the correct way, think of brushing the grass with the club-head, in the take-away and hitting area. This swing will help you create a wide backswing arc and swing the club into the ball on a low trajectory to ensure an extremely solid strike. The shot you hit will bore into the wind and stop fairly quickly on the green.

Jones's innovative shot-making skills helped him tame the wind at Hoylake and bring home the silver claret jug presented to the winner.

HIGH CUT

Jones was an accurate player, but like all golfers he was human. Some-times he would hit shots that missed the fairway and landed in rough grass, as was the case during the second U.S. Amateur qualifying round at Pennsylvania's Merion Cricket Club in 1930. Through experience, Jones learned that when the ball sits down in light rough, an inside-to-inside swing will not do the trick. That's because the clubhead usually gets snagged in the grass during the take-away, ultimately causing a faulty alignment with the ball at impact. A sharp-descending hit will not work either, because this technique causes the blades of grass to fill the grooves of the clubface and the ball to fly uncontrollably off the clubface some twenty yards farther than normal. Granted, if you could be ensured that the ball would always fly this same distance, you could compensate by taking two clubs less. The trouble is, you just never know how far the ball is going to fly from this type of lie in the rough. Therefore, the smartest strategy is to hit a Jones-style high-cut shot that hits the green, bounces gently to the right, and trickles toward the hole. Jones's ability to play this shot helped him win the last leg of the Slam at Merion.

When setting up to play the high cut, position the ball fairly forward in an exaggerated open stance. The open alignment promotes a more

In playing the high cut, swing the club on an upright plane.

upright out-to-in swing that, in turn, prevents the clubhead from getting snagged in the grass early in the backswing and imparts the desired cut-spin on the ball. Playing the ball up in the stance encourages you to keep your head and body well back through impact, which is critical to producing a high shot.

Cock the wrists early in the backswing and swing the club up steeply outside the target line.

On the downswing, release your right hand under your left instead of over it, since this allows you to work the clubface well underneath the ball. The ball will curve from left to right, fly extrahigh, work its way toward the pin from the left side of the green, and land softly on the green.

What You Can Learn from Bobby Jones

◆ On sharp dogleg-left holes, a supercontrolled power-draw shot is an advantage because it allows you to effectively shorten the hole and hit a more lofted club into the green.

◆ On extremely narrow par-four holes, consider playing a supercontrolled power fade, since this gentle left-to-right shot lands extrasoftly and is thus less apt to roll into rough bordering the fairway.

◆ To hit a solid wind-cheater shot, be sure to "chase" the ball with the clubhead through impact and employ a short finish.

◆ To enhance your control when hitting out of light rough, play the high, soft-landing cut shot by positioning the ball forward in your stance and swinging on an out-to-in path.

5 SHORT-GAME SCHOOL

*Mastering Jones's pitching, chipping, and putting
techniques will enable you to shoot lower scores*

Every pro who ever played the game, from Harry
Vardon to Ben Hogan, to Sam Snead, to Jack
Nicklaus, to Tiger Woods, understands that
developing a good pitching, chipping, and putting game
is the only true shortcut to shooting low scores. Jones
was a super short-game player, but unlike the aforesaid
great golfers he had his own simple, natural way of playing these shots.

Some golf aficionados and members of the press have
called Jones a genius as if he were born with the ability to
pitch the ball close to the cup, chip consistently well, and
putt the eyes out of the hole. And there is some truth to
their assessments. Jones was obviously born with soft
hands that helped his feel for distance. Nevertheless, his
short-game magic was developed more through practice.
Besides this, he learned from watching good players, particularly Maiden, make their way around Georgia's East
Lake course and Sarasota's Sara Bay course. Jones was

an ardent student of the game. No matter where he played, he watched
the techniques of others. Once alone, he would test a method of pitching, chipping, or putting out, and if he liked it, he usually added his own
nuances so that he felt even more comfortable. Let's now take a look at
how Jones hit the soft-landing pitch, the running chip, and solid on-line
putts.

THE PITCH

Jones obviously learned early on what many of the pros today, including
Greg Norman and Tiger Woods, are finding out. Hitting down on the
ball sharply in an attempt to make the ball carry a hazard, fly past the

One of Jones's secrets to playing the pitch was to choke down on the club a couple of inches to maximize control.

pin, and spin back toward the hole can be dangerous. In theory, this sounds like a smart strategy, but in fact it is not because the ball carries so much backspin that it often "dances" back off the green.

Jones believed that the most intelligent approach was to hit the ball cleanly off the turf, since he knew that by putting the clubface under the ball and taking advantage of its loft, he could hit a higher and softer pitch shot. This shot, played often by Jones during the 1926 British Open, really won him that championship.

In setting up for a pitch, Jones took an open stance, only spreading his feet about six inches apart, and played the ball well forward in the stance, somewhere between the left heel and left instep. Copy Jones, since the narrow stance will encourage an upright swing, and the forward ball position will enable you to get the full benefit of the clubface's loft, which is paramount to hitting soft-landing shots with a wedge. Also, grip the club lightly to promote lively hand action and choke down on the club a couple of inches to enhance your control.

On the backswing, leave your weight left and rock your left shoulder downward so you propel your arms and the club upward. Swing back until you feel your left shoulder rotate under your chin and your right wrist hinge due to the weight of the swinging clubhead. You don't want your backswing to be too short or else you will not create power and the acceleration needed to send the ball high into the air. You also want to create torque through a strong body coil, so keep your right foot firmly braced to prevent a sway of the body.

Start the downswing by rotating your knees toward the target. At this point in your swing, you should feel your right shoulder, your arms, and the club drop down dramatically, the left shoulder raising upward rapidly, and your head and upper body falling back. You are now perfectly poised to swing down and slide the clubface cleanly under the ball. Just unhinge your right wrist, accelerate the arms, and rotate your right hand under your left. Also, think about hitting through the ball with the clubface pointing toward the sky in the immediate follow-through, since this one swing thought will allow you to hold the face open and get the full value of the clubface's loft at impact.

The shot you hit will fly extrahigh and land extrasoftly even on firm greens.

THE CHIP

When chipping, Jones also set himself apart from his fellow competitors, who used only a very lofted club to play all sort of shots from the fringe. Many of today's tour professionals depend on the lofted sand wedge from around the green. This craze has now caught on, with many

No matter what club Jones chipped with, he always carefully looked over the terrain between the ball and the hole, trying to determine the subtle breaks in the green and the most ideal landing area.

golf instructors teaching students to choose the same club and learn a long, wristy swing to hit lofted chips and a short, wristless swing to hit running chips. This is unfortunate because average club-level golfers lack the talent and practice time to learn how to play these shots with a wedge. And it shows. I see players consistently either running the ball well past the pin, or hitting shots well short of the hole.

"I have found for myself that one club cannot be made to meet the exigencies of all kinds and length of chip shots," said Jones in *Bobby Jones on Golf.*

I believe that limiting yourself to one chipping club is a huge mistake because you do not give yourself a chance to chip the ball within easy one-putt range. The type of lie you are confronted with, the distance to a landing area, the lay of the land—sloping or level—between the ball and the hole, and finally the speed of the green vary greatly from course to course. These variables must always be considered when you face a chip shot. Even if you are blessed with soft hands and excellent hand-eye coordination, you are unlikely to evolve into a well-rounded chipper if you play all greenside shots with a sand wedge.

You will be better served by hitting chips Jones's way. He believed that the common dead-wristed stroke killed a golfer's chipping skill. He preferred loose wrists over firm wrists during the stroke to enhance his feel for the clubhead. And he certainly had perfect feel on the course, particularly en route to winning his first U.S. Open in 1923. During that championship, played at the Inwood Country Club on Long Island, New York, Jones played some magnificent chip shots off various lies using different clubs.

Jones also believed that on chip shots you should never loft the ball high into the air unless you absolutely have to. That is precisely why he played the club that would allow him to hit a low-flying shot that carried the fringe grass, landed near the edge of the green closest to him, and ran to the hole like a putt. Gary Player, one of only a few players who have won all four major championships, and a great chipper, agrees:

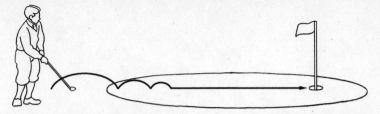

When chipping, Jones's goal was to land the ball on the edge of the green and let it run to the hole like a putt.

"Such a shot is easier to gauge because essentially you only have to deal with the element of roll versus air time and ground time."

No matter what club you choose to chip with, it's important that you take the time to focus on a precise landing spot, that you concentrate on determining what club is best for the shot, and that you stay positive. As a general rule, the longer the shot and the better the lie, the less lofted club you should choose.

In setting up to play chip shots like Jones, take an open stance and position your feet so close together that they nearly touch. Play the ball opposite your right toe with your hands a few inches ahead of the ball.

On the backswing, keep both feet firmly planted on the ground as you make a compact swing and allow the wrists to hinge freely. Stop when the clubshaft is parallel to the ground at waist level, the toe of the club points toward the sky, and your wrists have hinged fully.

On the downswing, unhinge your wrists. Let the right hand and forearm rotate counterclockwise through impact so that the clubface closes slightly and you impart a small degree of hook-spin on the ball. Hitting the ball with this kind of spin was one of Jones's secrets. This type of spin makes the ball roll faster, which is exactly why you can make such a short backswing and still reach the hole.

In setting up to chip, consider playing the ball off the right foot the way Jones did.

PUTTING

In his prime, Jones was an exceptionally good putter, and what intrigued onlookers was the way he set up to the ball and swung his famous Calamity Jane putter. Unlike other fine players of his day, Jones did not believe in standing erect at address, with both arms extended and the eyes directly over the ball. He also did not believe in employing a straight-back and straight-through stroke and keeping the face of the putter dead square to the target line on the backswing and downswing.

Jones crouched down low because this gave him better leverage and more control over the stroke. He pointed both elbows outward because he claimed this helped him alleviate body tension and make a smooth stroke. Both Arnold Palmer and Jack Nicklaus, two of the all-time best putters, adopted Jones's crouched-over, elbows-out style of putting.

Jones also kept his eyes inside the target line because this position

In addressing a putt, Jones set his eyes inside the target line, instead of directly over the ball, to promote an inside-square-inside stroke

helped him employ a putting stroke similar to the normal swing he used to hit woods and irons. The putter's head swung along an inside path on the backswing, returned square to the ball at impact, then swung back to the inside in the follow-through.

Jones was fairly conventional regarding the aspects of the grip. Just like many of his contemporaries, he draped his left forefinger over his right pinky and third finger as this provided him with a sense of security in the hands. However, unlike them, he set his left thumb straight down the shaft to help the left hand control the path of the club and his right

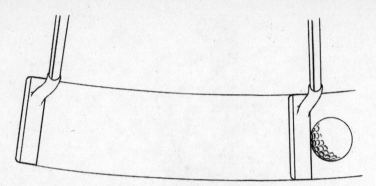

If a straight-back-straight-through stroke is not working for you, swing the putter back well inside the target line, just as Jones did.

thumb down the side of the shaft to help the right hand control the power of the stroke.

In completing his setup, Jones played the ball opposite his left heel, with the hands slightly ahead of it. These aspects of Jones's address are conventional, too. You cannot say the same about his actual putting action, yet it worked wonders, especially during the 1925 U.S. Amateur final against his friend Watts Gunn, which Jones won by a huge 8-and-7 margin. The most inspiring birdie putts Jones sank were on hole number one and hole number two of the afternoon round. These got him going and laid the groundwork for his decisive victory.

On the backswing, Jones let his wrists hinge so freely that the club was lifted well off the ground and swung well to the inside. In contrast, his fellow players kept their wrists firm during the backswing, swung the putter's head back low to the ground, and maintained a square clubface position. To others, Jones's method was highly unorthodox, yet it made perfectly good sense to Jones because swinging the putter along the same inside path as normal allowed him to be more comfortable and confident.

On the downswing, Jones unhinged his right wrist to help him return the club from an open position to a square position at impact. To get a better sense of this movement, think of a door opening and closing.

Jones unhinged his wrists on the downswing to return the club to a
square through-impact position and only looked up after the hit.

In staying faithful to his unconventional swing technique, Jones
also rotated his right hip and right knee toward the target, rather than
keeping the lower body frozen. This free and fluid right-sided action
aided the rhythm of the stroke, particularly on long putts, and also
ensured that the putterhead returned low to the ground in a more
streamlined fashion. Had Jones kept the lower body locked, he would
probably have chopped down on the ball and not swept through it so
smoothly.

When you consider that surveys by leading golf magazines show that recreational players three-putt an average of four times per round, it's time for players—maybe you, too—to start switching to a Jones-type putting method that is easy to repeat and more natural feeling than the robotlike stiff-wristed swing.

Before closing, I must tell you that Ben Crenshaw, one of golf's all-time best players on the greens, adopted a Jones-like method after joining the PGA Tour, and that's one chief reason why he has been so successful. Crenshaw has won tournaments all over the world, but most recognizably the 1984 and 1995 Masters. Crenshaw's success shows that Jones was ahead of his time in developing a virtual foolproof stroke—one so foolproof that it will allow Crenshaw to return to the winner's circle when he joins the Senior PGA Tour.

What You Can Learn from Bobby Jones

◆ When playing a short pitch, pick the ball cleanly off the turf, taking a shallow divot by accelerating your arms through the impact zone.

◆ The most vital secrets to good chipping are playing the ball opposite your right foot to promote early contact, allowing the right wrist to hinge freely on the backswing to enhance clubhead feel, and closing the clubface slightly through impact to impart a slight degree of hook-spin to the ball.

◆ To promote a consistent stroke and on-line putts, point both elbows out at address.

◆ On long putts, rotate your right hip and right knee toward the target; this lower-body action will enhance the rhythm of your stroke and give you the little bit of added power you need to roll the ball all the way to the hole.

6 HIGH-LEVEL MANAGEMENT

Jones's on-course mental strategies will help you avoid making costly mistakes

In rating the smartest golfers of all time, Bobby Jones is definitely high on my list. Jones realized early on in his golfing life that there is much more to the game than just hitting the ball powerfully off the tee, accurately on approach shots, near the hole from around the green, and into the cup from on the putting surface. To become a good golfer and reach your scoring potential, you must be able to think strategically and plan out your round. In addressing this golfing fact, here's what Tiger Woods's former coach John Anselmo said:

"It's one thing to be at the wheel of a Ferrari, it's another thing to be able to maneuver the car around a track so intelligently that you negotiate the curves, out-think fellow drivers, avoid an accident, and cross the finish line first." Unquestionably, Jones had the Ferrari of golf swings and an uncanny ability to maneuver his way around the golf course.

Golf is not just a matter of employing a good swing and evolving into an expert shot-maker. You truly must

The intensity in Jones's eyes shows that a high percentage of the game is played between the ears.

think before you act, from the time you tee up on hole number one until you sink your final putt on hole number eighteen. A lapse in concentration at the wrong time, a negative image, an overly aggressive shot, or an error in assessing yardage, wind speed, or the lie can cost you. You constantly have to be on your toes when playing the course, particularly in a stroke-play event, but also in a match-play event.

The reason why Jones beat "Old Man Par" so often and won so many championships was because he also did such an excellent job of managing his mind, his body, and the course. Let's now take a closer look at these skills and the elements involved.

OFF THE TEE

Jones never made the mistake of taking a driver out of his bag and hitting his characteristic draw shot just because he was playing a par-four or par-five hole. He assessed the hole first, as you should.

Proceeding with caution is one of the most important elements of strategic golf. Start by looking at the hole's shape first. If it curves to the left and your normal shot is a fade, consider hitting a draw since this will essentially shorten the hole and allow you to play a more lofted iron into the green. The more lofted the club, the easier it is to hit and the more likely you are to land the ball close to the hole. Having said this, before deciding on the draw, determine if the added yardage you will pick up, due to the right-to-left spin imparted on the ball, could send the ball into water or another severe hazard. If so, go with your bread-and-butter fade and just accept having to play a slightly longer shot into the green. By the same token, sometimes a solidly hit drive will run through the corner of the dogleg into trouble. In this case, a smarter strategy may be to play a straight shot with a fairway wood or long iron off the tee to ensure hitting the fairway.

If you decide to play a straight shot off the tee, hit from the center of the teeing area to open up the hole. When playing a draw, tee the ball up on the far left side of the tee and aim down the right side of the fairway so the ball curves back toward its center. When playing a fade, tee up near the right-side tee marker and aim left. On short par-four holes that feature steep downhill slopes beyond the landing area, consider hitting an iron off the tee and laying back to ensure a shot off a level lie.

APPROACH SHOTS

The first order of business in playing an iron-approach shot into the green is to assess the lie. How your ball sits in the grass has a big bearing on club selection and whether you should aim for the flagstick or the *fat* of the green, that large expanse of green to the left or right side of the hole. This is exactly what Jones did on the final hole of the play-off with Bobby Cruickshank, when competing for the 1923 U.S. Open. Even though his ball was in light rough, 190 yards from the hole, and he had to carry a water hazard, Jones determined that the lie allowed him to be aggressive with a long iron and attack the flag. Jones's shot landed six feet from the cup, allowing him to clinch the championship.

If the ball sits cleanly on fairway grass, the lie is level, the flagstick is in the middle of the green, and you feel confident that you have correctly matched a club to the distance of the shot, make a smooth swing and attack the flag.

If, on the other hand, the lie is bad, the flagstick is close to a hazard, and you are confused about club selection, you should play more cautiously. Incidentally, regarding picking the right club, don't think this is something only top pros can handle. If you have determined through practice the average distance you hit each club, selection is just a matter of simple mathematics. Simply subtract the distance of your drive from the yardage of the par-four or par-five hole you're playing, then choose the club you hit the remaining distance.

When selecting a club, be careful not to let your ego get in the way. Many amateurs fall into the trap of trying to stretch a club beyond its limitations just to be macho. If you make the same mistake, you're likely to overswing, speed up your tempo, and hit a misdirected shot. If you're confused—for example, caught between playing a smooth 9-iron or a hard pitching wedge—go with the 9-iron. Playing the less lofted club is always the smartest strategy. The reason is, even if you hit the ball over the green, you'll face a fairly easy chip because the majority of sand traps and water hazards are usually situated to the sides of the green. As Jones said in the book *The Bobby Jones Story*, "I never try to force a club."

Doing battle with the ego is not the only reason you should make adjustments in club selection. In playing a shot off a downhill lie, the effective loft of the club will be decreased at impact. For example, an 8-iron will act like a 7-iron. So, if the distance calls for an 8-iron, play the more lofted 9-iron. Off uphill lies, the effective loft of the club will increase, so play a stronger club—e.g., a 7-iron instead of an 8-iron.

When hitting shots to greens above or below you, you also must make adjustments in club selection. If the green sits well above the level of the tee, take at least one more club. On shots to a green below you, take at least one club less.

In dealing with heavy rough, it's usually a smart idea to take a more lofted club and aim for the middle of the green, as Jones did.

When the grass bordering the fairway is not particularly thick or high, it will offer far less resistance to the clubhead in the impact area, so that you hit a "flyer." What this means is that because blades of grass intervene between the ball and the clubface at impact, you produce a shot with less backspin. The ball shoots up into the air at a faster rate, flies about twenty yards farther than normal, and rolls more, too. Therefore, if you see signs of a flyer when addressing the ball, compensate by taking less club and aim for the biggest portion of the green.

When the rough is severe, and the ball is sitting down deeply in it, take your medicine and play out safely to the fairway rather than go for the green. This strategy may make you feel like you're wasting a shot, but once in the fairway you can still save par with a good iron shot and putt.

Another shot that calls for caution is from a fairway bunker with a high lip, on a par-five hole. Hitting a solid dive and having the ball bounce into a fairway bunker can be upsetting. But if you use your head and play an iron down the fairway, rather than try to hit a miracle shot with a wood and run the risk of hitting the lip, you can still make par or even birdie. Only if the lie is clean and the lip is low should you play aggressively.

If you face a fairway shot from a low-lipped bunker, on a par-four hole, and you are iron distance from the green, go for the green. That's what Jones did in the 1926 British Open played at Royal Lytham & St. Annes. Through seventeen holes of the final round Jones was tied with Al Waltrous. Waltrous hit first and put the pressure on Jones by hitting a drive down the center of the fairway. Jones hit his drive into a fairway bunker, situated approximately 175 yards from the hole. Waltrous, first to play his approach shot, hit the ball onto the green. The pressure was on Jones. He responded by hitting a lofted iron shot over the dunes and onto the green, inside Watrous's ball. Jones pulled off this shot by concentrating on the one thing that's necessary when hitting an iron out of a fairway bunker: he hit the ball cleanly—ball first, sand second. To ensure this type of contact, play the ball forward in the stance, make a more upright swing than normal, keep your head behind the ball in the impact zone, and hit the ball on the upswing.

AROUND THE GREEN

When hitting chips and short pitch shots from around the green, Jones was careful to analyze the lie of the ball, the distance to the landing spot on the edge of the green closest to him, the area, whether flat or sloping, between the ball and the hole, the speed of the green, and the distance to the pin. This preswing process, plus visualizing in his mind how certain shots hit with different clubs would react in the air and on the ground, allowed him to pick the proper club for the job. Any good course manager, amateur or pro, goes through this same routine.

Once you choose a club, take a couple of practice swings to get a feel for the shot and to instill a strong sense of confidence. Next, focus your eyes back and fourth a couple of times, from ball to target, so you get a sense of the distance and the length of the shot and the speed of swing needed.

Finally, make a smooth swing that is a facsimile of your smooth practice swing.

ON THE GREEN

Jones was such a keen observer on the course that he started analyzing the breaks in a green before even arriving on it to putt. After hitting an approach, Jones walked toward the green, all the time looking carefully at the slopes on its surface and determining how the water would drain off. This careful analysis will allow you to get a good idea of the breaks in a green. Look carefully at nearby bodies of water, too, as the ball always breaks toward water. To further read the breaks, look at the ball from behind it, behind the hole, and both sides of the hole. If you are still confused, *plumb-bob* the line to determine the break, in the following manner:

Stand with your body at a right angle to the horizon and hold the putter at arm's length in front of you with only your thumb and forefinger securing the top of the grip. Block out the view of the ball with the lower part of the putter's shaft, then close your nondominant eye. If the shaft now appears to also obscure the hole, the putt is straight. If the shaft appears to be to the right of the hole, the putt will break from right to left. If the shaft falls to the left of the hole, the putt will break from left to right.

As Jones learned, the grain in the green should also be a consideration when preparing to putt. If the grass has a shiny look, the grain is running toward the hole, so stroke the ball easier to make a shorter putting stroke. If the green's surface is dull, the grain is running away from the ball, toward you, so stroke the putt more firmly to reach the hole.

BETWEEN SHOTS

Lee Trevino, former U.S. Open, PGA, and British Open winner had the ability to joke around in between shots, then turn on the concentration button the split second he got over a shot. Tiger Woods used to be a little like this, I guess because kidding around with his caddy Steve Williams helped him relax. The thing is, he doesn't joke around much anymore, and certainly not while competing in any one of the four major championships. It seemed Tiger was getting lax because of the joking, so that when the time came to hit a shot, he wasn't as focused as he should have been. This makes sense, because as Jones said in *Bobby Jones on Golf*:

"One lapse of concentration, one bit of carelessness, is more disastrous than a number of mechanical mistakes, mainly because it is harder to bring the mind back to the business at hand than it is to correct or guard against a physical mistake recognized as soon as it appears."

Jones and other great players of the game, most notably Sam Snead, Arnold Palmer, Jack Nicklaus, and Tom Watson, never let themselves get out of a mental cocoon of concentration for too long between shots, particularly putts. Jones almost always focused on something, usually the ball or the target. However, he did not believe in being overly stoic from the start of the round to its finish, like Ben Hogan or Severiano Ballesteros during their heyday.

Unlike Ballesteros, who entered a bubble of intense concentration, or Hogan, who kept silent during the round, Jones sometimes talked to his playing partners to relieve tension. I believe you will make fewer errors and score better if you concentrate on the shot at hand and save the joking for the nineteenth hole after the round. But, by the same token, stay fairly "loose," otherwise you will get mentally tired according to Jones.

CONFIDENCE

Jones realized that confidence was indispensable to first-class golf and that one sure way to developing it is perfectly matching a set of clubs to your body shape and strengths, plus your natural swing tendencies. Yes, a club perfectly suited to you can actually help you swing more efficiently and increase your confidence.

I believe wholeheartedly that many physically strong golfers would swing better and hit more solid shots by switching from extrastiff-shafted clubs to soft-steel- or graphite-shafted clubs. If you laugh at this suggestion, consider that Butch Harmon, Tiger Woods's present coach, a strong individual, swings irons featuring soft-flex shafts. These are similar to Jones's hickory-shafted "sticks" because they promote better feel and timing. I might add that Harmon is very strong and could swing extrastiff shafts if he wanted to.

If you presently swing clubs with extrastiff shafts and your shots tend to drift off to the right of target, improve your swing, confidence, and shots by making a switch to more flexible shafts.

FORTITUDE

To be a winner, you must learn how to brush off a bad shot or bad hole and immediately focus on the next shot or hole you're playing. When Jones was young, he was known for cursing, throwing clubs, or ripping up scorecards in the middle of the round. Unfortunately, this kind of attitude hurts your game, as Jones realized.

To promote good scores, adopt a what's-done-is-done attitude and concentrate on staying in the present, playing one shot at a time to the best of your ability. Moreover, emotionally, try to stay on an even keel, never letting yourself get overly excited about a good shot or overly down about a bad shot. Take the time to relax and prepare for the shot, so that you arrive at the ball ready to devote 100 percent to the course situation and swing.

ENERGY

On the day of competition, Jones made sure he ate breakfast, albeit a light one, to ensure that he retained his strength and stayed mentally alert from the start of the round to its finish.

The smartest idea is to start the day with a piece of toast, a bowl of cereal, a glass of juice, then energize yourself between shots at different stages of the round. Energy bars, fruit, chocolate, water, and Gatorade are all good sources. You really hungry players can try following in the footsteps of Senior PGA Tour player Al Geiberger—Mr. 59—who ate peanut-butter-and-jelly sandwiches enroute to winning the 1966 PGA championship.

Warning: Stay away from coffee because of the caffeine. The last thing you want to feel is jittery over shots.

What You Can Learn from Bobby Jones

◆ If the hole you're playing is short, or there is a chance you could reach a water hazard down the fairway, consider hitting a fairway wood or long iron off the tee.

◆ When hitting a draw, tee up on the left side of the teeing area.

◆ When hitting a fade, tee up on the right side of the teeing area.

◆ Assess the lie and the landing area before you decide to attack the flag on an approach shot.

◆ Visualize different shots hit with different clubs, and "see" how the ball reacts in the air and on the ground to help you choose the correct club and hit the right chip shot.

◆ To help you read the break in a green, determine where water would drain off its surface. This preswing procedure will help you pinpoint the slopes in the putting surface and hit a good-breaking putt.

◆ When walking to the ball, start planning out your next shot.

◆ Forget a bad shot, so you can give your next shot 100 percent concentration.

7 PRACTICAL PRACTICE

Jones's priority on the practice tee was to pinpoint a swing fault and fix it

Bobby Jones was a lot like the son of a Kentucky Derby winner, in that he came from good stock yet still needed to follow a rigorous training schedule to develop good skills and stay in good form.

I don't feel uncomfortable comparing Jones to a race-horse because, in fact, he was a top thoroughbred who looked graceful swinging any golf club. And, though he may have been gifted, he took the time to develop a set of proven setup and swing fundamentals while, as you have already learned, adding his own nuances in the same way a chef dresses up a dish with a little more of this and that. Having said this, please don't think that Jones was such an unorthodox player that only he could employ the complex movements of his swing. Rather, he worked within the boundaries of the basics, but tweaked them to find the most natural swing possible, a technique that each and every golfer can clone provided he or she devotes time to practice.

When Jones practiced, his only goal was to pinpoint a fault and fix it.

Jones was proud of his swing and highly confident it would produce solidly hit, well-placed shots out on the course under championship conditions. That's because he had spent so much time working out any kinks in practice. Consequently, he knew his swing inside out and was able to fix it when it was out of sync. It's important that you learn and feel the position of the club at all points of the backswing and downswing so that you can repeat a good swing and sense and correct a fault.

Jones hated to practice hitting shots with clubs that he was handling well on the course. Besides, he believed that if you tinkered too much with a good technique, you'd inevitably find a way to make it a bad technique. I share that opinion, particularly after witnessing former great champions, among them Curtis Strange and Nick Faldo, fall off professional golf's radar screen because they became obsessed with making swing changes for really no reason at all, except, perhaps, to try to make a good technique perfect. As sports psychologist Bob Rotella says, "Golf is not a game of perfect."

Jones usually only worked on his swing after he had detected a fault on the course, wanting to fix it as soon as possible. For example, if he felt that unhinging the right wrist early on the downswing caused him to hit off-line shots during a round, he would work on swinging the right elbow down into his side. This one action causes the hands, arms, and club to drop down automatically while the right wrist stays hinged until a split second before impact when the speed of the swing is ready to reach a crescendo.

There's no doubt that, like Jones, you will find value in practicing several types of shots and hitting various irons to various targets from various angles. However, you will also get enjoyment out of analyzing your game after the round, pinpointing a fault, and correcting the problem. Let me educate you on the common causes of common faults and provide you with easy-to-follow corrective measures. After all, Jones believed the secret to beneficial practice was to keep working on specific problems. Here's how Jones elaborated on this subject:

"If you cannot think of some kink to iron out or some fault to correct, don't practice. And if there is a kink or a fault, as soon as it has been found and cured, stop immediately and don't run the risk of unearthing a new one or exaggerating the cure until it becomes a blemish itself."

DRIVER SWING PROBLEMS

Problem #1

The Sway *(You sway when you move the body laterally away from the target, in such an exaggerated fashion that weight shifts onto the outside of the right foot, you lose your balance, and you usually hit a top shot.)*

COMMON CAUSE: The player tries too hard to shift weight to the right foot and leg on the backswing.

Practical Practice Solution

Jones recommended that the player set his weight on the insides of the feet at address, but I offer two other remedies:

1. Point your right foot directly at the target line; this minor address adjustment allows you to keep your weight on the inside of your right foot during the backswing and promotes a stronger body coil.

2. Practice with a golf ball lodged under the right side of your right instep.

Problem #2

The Reverse Pivot *(You reverse when you shift weight to your left foot on the backswing and right foot on the downswing. The end result of a reverse pivot is usually a weak slice.)*

COMMON CAUSE: The player tilts his or her head toward the left shoulder instead of waiting for the left shoulder to turn under a steady chin.

Practical Practice Solution

Take a lesson from Jones. He kept his left eye focused on the back of the ball until his hips and shoulders had turned.

Problem #3

Exaggerated Flat Swing Path *(The swing path is overly flat when the club swings well behind the body early in the takeaway. This fault usually causes you to either hit the ball well right of target or, sensing this, close the clubface and hit a duck-hook shot left of target.)*

COMMON CAUSE: The player consciously pulls the club inside the target line because he or she has been taught that the club must swing along an inside path on the backswing rather than straight back.

Practical Practice Solution

The club must swing to the inside slightly, but not due to any conscious manipulation on your part. Do what Jones did: let the clockwise turning action of the shoulders start the club moving inside.

To prove to yourself turning the shoulders does control the inside swing of the club, rest the toe end of a 5-iron against the baseboard of a wall in your home, then turn your shoulders. Note how the club swings away from the wall, on the inside, automatically.

Problem #4

Exaggerated Upright Swing Plane *(The club swings straight up into the air instead of moving back low to the ground until weight starts to shift to your right foot. From such a steep at-the-top position, the tendency is to pull the club straight down into the ball and hit with a chopping rather than sweeping action.)*

COMMON CAUSE: When playing a driver, the player positions the ball back too far in the stance—midway between the feet—with the hands several inches ahead of the ball. This setup tends to force the player to hinge the wrists dramatically in the take-away and swing up on an overly steep plane.

Practical Practice Solution

Copy Jones. He positioned the ball well forward in the stance with his hands slightly behind it. Also, groove a passive-wrists take-away action by working on the following drill:

Take your new setup position for a driver and place a second ball along the target line, between twelve and eighteen inches behind the ball you're addressing. Keeping your eyes on the back of the front ball, swing the driver back along the target line, just above the ground. If you make a smooth sweeping action in the take-away, the back of the clubhead will knock the second ball backward. Incorporate this kind of action into your normal driver swing and you'll be less apt to pick the club straight up into the air and more apt to hit powerfully accurate shots—Jones style!

Problem #5

Lateral Leg Lunge *(You lunge when you drive the legs vigorously toward the target at the start of the downswing. This fault forces the clubface into an open position at impact with a slice shot resulting.)*

COMMON CAUSE: The player tries to consciously shift weight over to the left foot and leg at the start of the downswing.

Practical Practice Solution

Replant the ball of your left foot and shift your hips laterally as Jones did at the start of the downswing. Next, concentrate on rotating the hips counterclockwise so weight shifts to the left foot and leg automatically. That way, you will be poised to return the clubface square to the ball at impact and hit a straight shot.

Problem #6

Over-the-Top Move *(You come over the top when you let the right shoulder jut outward and raise up high above the left shoulder on the downswing. In doing this, you will likely hit a pull-slice shot, with the ball starting left and curving right.)*

COMMON CAUSE: The player tries too hard to hit the ball instead of swinging the club.

Practical Practice Solution

Concentrate on letting your lower body play the lead role on the downswing, as Jones did. Also, repeat the following words to yourself before you step into the shot to take your address: *Swing the force, don't force the swing.*

IRON GAME SHOT-MAKING PROBLEMS

Problem #1

Heavy Hitting *(You hit the ball heavy or "fat" when you dig the club into the turf behind the ball.)*

COMMON CAUSE: The player believes the secret to imparting backspin on the ball is taking a divot of turf, so he swings the club up and down on a steep plane and pulls the club down hard.

Practical Practice Solution

To avoid hitting heavy shots, while at the same time imparting backspin on the ball, practice timing the unhinging action of the wrists on the downswing so that you can snap the club into the ball first. Yes, you cut out the divot of turf *after* striking the ball first. That's what Jones did, which is precisely why he did not hit "flyers" and had such good distance control with the irons.

Problem #2

Shanking *(The shank is a shot that flies practically immediately right of target. You hit a shank when the hosel or "shank" rather than the center of the clubface or "sweet spot" makes contact with the ball.)*

COMMON CAUSE: Jones believed the most common cause of the shank was failing to retain the hinged angle in the wrists on the downswing. This fault causes the player to shove the club at the ball and swing across the target line with the hosel, shank, or neck of the club leading.

Practical Practice Solution

After making a longer backswing action and allowing your wrists to hinge freely, replant your left foot the way Jones did so that your hands and club drop downward automatically and you make square contact with the ball.

Problem #3

Thin Hits *(You hit the ball thin when the clubface's leading edge contacts the top portion of the ball.)*

COMMON CAUSE: In an attempt to make a clean upswing hit and sweep the ball off the turf, the player keeps the majority of his weight on his right foot and leg through impact and uses his hands to slap at the ball.

Practical Practice Solution

Rotate the right knee toward the target as Jones did early on in the downswing to ensure a good weight shift and let centrifugal force whip the club into the back of the ball.

SHORT-GAME FAULTS

Problem #1

Weak Pitch Shots from Rough *(You feel yourself losing acceleration through impact and hit shots that fall well short of target.)*

COMMON CAUSE: The player sets the clubhead down in the grass behind the ball, keeps his weight equally balanced on both feet, and tries to hit the ball with a scooping action.

Practical Practice Solution

Hold the club above the grass behind the ball to prevent a snagging problem, play the ball back in the stance with the hands ahead as Jones did, and keep 60 percent of your weight on your left foot to promote a sharp hit on the descent. Additionally, practice shots out of shallow divots, since this will help you to learn to hit with a descending blow.

Problem #2

Pulling the Ball on Pitch Shots *(You pull the ball when you hit a shot that flies straight but left of target. What's frustrating and puzzling is that, often, you feel you did everything right— employed an even take-away action, turned the shoulders, shifted weight to the right side on the backswing, and made a smooth downswing—yet you still hit a pull. That's because the fault is not with your swing, but your setup.)*

COMMON CAUSE: The player aligns his feet and body well left of target, then points the club in the same direction.

Practical Practice Solution

Set the club down first, squarely to the ball and the target, then jockey your feet and body into position, just as Jones used to do when playing competitive golf. Then ask a friend or your local pro to stand behind you and check your alignment.

If you face a blind pitch shot or simply have trouble aligning yourself to the hole, pick out an interim target, say a bare spot in the grass about three feet in front of the ball and directly in line with the flagstick. Next, align your clubface perpendicular to your secondary target spot, then your body parallel to the ball–interim-target line. This preswing procedure will encourage you to groove a good setup.

Problem #3

Poor Distance Control on Short Pitch Shots *(You hit short pitch shots over the green.)*

COMMON CAUSE: The player, while trying to hit a short pitch over a hazard to a tight pin, swings the club on an overly flat plane.

Practical Practice Solution

To promote added feel for the club and shot, hold the club more lightly than normal, about four on a one-to-ten scale that measures grip pressure. Hinge the wrists freely as Jones did on the backswing to help you swing the club up on an upright angle, and turn your right hand under your left through impact. Learning this technique will help you lift the ball nicely into the air so it carries the hazard and stops quickly next to the hole.

Problem #4

Poor Directional Control on Chip Shots *(You either hit chips well right or left of target.)*

COMMON CAUSE: The player fails to guide the club through the ball with the left hand, so that its face finishes square to the hole at impact and the ball rolls directly at the hole.

Practical Practice Solution

To keep the club square through impact and hit accurate chips, keep your head locked in position and your eyes focused on the ball. These two simple swing keys helped

Jones make contact with the ball consistently and hit the shot the same way virtually every time with a particular club.

Gripping the club more firmly with the last three fingers of your left hand—the chipping swing's guide hand—will also aid your control.

Additionally, employ a reverse overlap grip by draping your left forefinger over the first three fingers of your right hand. This unique hold will provide you with even more security, so that you keep the clubface and the shot under control.

Problem #5

Lack of Confidence on Chip Shots *(When you lose confidence over the ball, you feel uncomfortable, you tend to rush the shot or look up before impact and hit some type of bad shot.)*

COMMON CAUSE: The player fails to understand that proper planning prevents poor performance and instills confidence.

Practical Practice Solution
Develop a regular chip-shot routine similar to Jones's. When practicing chipping, start by analyzing the lie carefully. Next, stare at the hole to get a better feel for distance. Next, before choosing a club, wait until you see a chipping swing work well in your mind's eye and the shot fly and roll toward the hole. Next, make a fluid practice swing to rehearse your technique. Take this same routine to the course and you will feel confident about your chances of hitting shots close to the cup.

Problem #6

Short Putt "Yip" *(You "yip" a putt when you make an extrashort, quick stroke and fail to deliver the putter's face square to the hole at impact.)*

COMMON CAUSE: The player is anxious over the putt for fear of missing the hole from such a short distance and feeling embarrassed. This fear can be traced to previous missed putts due to overconcern with the degree of break in the green. The player prefers to "miss it quick" as teachers say, just to get over the fear.

Practical Practice Solution

On putts of three feet and less, play for no break, as Jones often did. Plan to stroke the ball firmly into the back of the cup. Furthermore, to keep your mind off missing and on holing out, imagine the ball hitting an imaginary bull's-eye of a target located at the back of the hole.

Problem #7

Hitting Weak Long Putts *(You leave the ball short of the hole on long putts.)*

COMMON CAUSE: The player decelerates the putter in the hitting area or stabs at the ball in the impact area.

Practical Practice Solution

Let your right wrist hinge on the backswing, then unhinge in the impact zone, as Jones's did, to enhance your feel for the clubhead and put some speed in the stroke.

Another way to cure your problem is to place a dime down on the practice green, approximately three inches in front of the ball. Swing through, trying to brush the dime with the bottom of the putterhead. This drill will encourage you to swing through the ball rather than at it, accelerate the putter, and hit the ball up to the hole. Now simply incorporate this newfound technique into your existing putting stroke.

What You Can Learn from Bobby Jones

◆ Practicing with a purpose, not just beating balls at the driving range, is the only shortcut to good golf.

◆ Go to the range with a specific goal in mind, such as fixing a sway problem in your swing.

◆ Hit shots with clubs that give you trouble, not your favorite ones in the bag.

◆ To cure an overly flat swing plane, practice letting the turning action of your shoulders automatically bring the club inside the target line the right amount.

◆ If you hit thin iron shots, concentrate on shifting your weight over to your left side on the downswing. This singular key will allow you to stay down through impact and hit solid shots.

◆ Follow a set routine to raise your level of confidence on chip shots.

◆ If you get jittery on short, breaking putts and employ a nervous "yip" stroke, aim for the back of the cup and hit the ball firmly.

Afterword

After making history by winning the Grand Slam in 1930, Jones retired from competitive golf, but by no means gave up the game. In fact, he immersed himself in golf with the priority of giving back something special to the sport he loved so much.

Shortly after retirement, Jones made Hollywood instructional movies in conjunction with Warner Brothers that were shown in theaters across the country. He also wrote newspaper articles and books, served as a golf ambassador by speaking on radio, and designed clubs for the A. C. Spalding Co. And if that was not enough, Jones, along with Scottish architect Alister Mackenzie, designed the Augusta National Golf Club's championship course, which, since 1934, has been the permanent venue in Augusta, Georgia, for the Masters, one of professional golf's four coveted major championships. Although Mackenzie is the designer on record, it is obvious from the final creation—with its elevated, crowned greens, strategically placed bunkers, and manicured collection areas bordering the putting surfaces—that Jones played a huge role in the design. It's obvious, too, that Jones was influenced by Donald Ross–designed courses he had played and loved, such as Pinehurst in Pinehurst, North Carolina, and Sara Bay in Sarasota, Florida.

The golf professionals who have competed at Augusta and continue to compete there every year owe great thanks to Jones and his Wall Street friend Clifford Roberts. Roberts played a major role in the original development of the club, its ongoing membership, and until 1977 hosted the prestigious Masters—the tournament many professionals, including Jack Nicklaus, call their favorite. Jones played in that championship until 1947 when his health began to fail.

Jones was the player Nicklaus and so many other golfers and non-golfers admired for his poetic swing, creative shot-making game, character, courage, intellect, and devotion. Even after 1968, when a spinal disease left Jones paralyzed, he managed to maintain his dignity.

Jones passed on in 1971. Nevertheless, he left a legacy like no other. Golfers will remember, for a long time to come, the great swing that won him thirteen of the twenty-seven major championships he entered, and, too, the personality of this man that won him so many friends around the world.

I feel honored to have connected to Jones through an in-depth analysis of his techniques. You can bet that you will take away something special from this book—what I believe are the true swing, shot-making, practice, and strategic secrets of one of history's most dominating players, and your link to improvement. You can bet, too, that up in heaven they simply call Robert Tyre Jones *Champ*. He will be that, and more, for eternity.

Index

John Andrisani writes for various golf and nongolf publications, including *American Golf Pro*, *Golf Digest* (Japan), and *Playboy* magazines. The former senior instruction editor at *GOLF Magazine* is the author of numerous instruction books, most notably *The Tiger Woods Way* and *The Hogan Way*. Andrisani is a low-handicap golfer and former winner of the World Golf Writers' Championship.

Shu Kuga is an award-winning artist specializing in golf. His lifelike illustrations appear regularly in top golf magazines and golf books published worldwide.

Yasuhiro Tanabe is a freelance photographer whose book credits include the *Complete Idiot's Guide to Improving Your Short Game* by Jim McLean and *A-Game Golf* by John Anselmo with John Andrisani.